WINNING CASINO BLACKJACK for the NON-COUNTER

"His candor . . . is refreshing in its honesty . . . For the casual player who is not inclined to devote the time necessary for mastering a count strategy, this is the best book I've seen of its type."

ARNOLD SNYDER
Blackjack Author
Publisher of Blackjack Forum

"I've seen all the best, and Avery Cardoza ranks as one of the greatest blackjack players in the world. This book will make any beginning player a winner."

EDWIN SILBERSTANG
Foremost Gambling Authority in America
Author of Over 20 Gaming Titles

To My Father

ABOUT THE AUTHOR

Avery Cardoza is considered one of the greatest blackjack players in the world, and is feared by the major casinos, none of which will knowingly deal cards to him. He is the best-selling author of more than a dozen gambling books and advanced strategies including one of the most important gambling books ever written, the encyclopedic *How to Win at Gambling*, and the best-selling classic, *Casino Craps for the Winner*.

Cardoza has always made his living from gambling (never having held a 9-5 job) and has parlayed his winnings into a publishing empire whose best-selling and important gaming books can be found throughout the United States and in over 50 countries around the world.

Though originally from New York City, where he is occasionally found, Cardoza has used his winnings to pursue a lifestyle of extensive travelling which has included extended sojourns in such exotic locales as Bahia in Brazil, Jerusalem and Tokyo, as well as California, South Florida, New Orleans, and of course, Las Vegas, where he did extensive research into the mathematical, emotional and psychological aspects of winning.

In this book, Cardoza has put it all together, his years of professional play, teaching, research and knowledge, to teach the player the concepts and strategies of winning play.

WINNING CASINO BLACKJACK for the NON-COUNTER

Avery Cardoza

- Gambling Research Institute -
Cardoza Publishing

Cardoza Publishing, publisher of **Gambling Research Institute** (GRI) books, is the foremost gaming and gambling publisher in the world with a library of more than 45 up-to-date and easy-to-read books and strategies.

These authoritative works are written by the top experts in their fields and with more than 3,500,000 books in print, represent the best-selling and most popular gaming books anywhere.

Printing History

First Printing	*November 1981*
Second Printing	*February 1982*
Third Printing	*July 1982*
Fourth Printing	*May 1984*
Fifth Printing	*July 1985*
Sixth Printing	*September 1986*
Seventh Printing	*October 1988*
Eight Printing	*January 1990*

New Revised Edition

First Printing	*June 1992*

Library of Congress Catalog Card No: 92-70387
ISBN: 0-940685-23-X
Cover Photos by Ron Charles

CARDOZA PUBLISHING
P.O. Box 1500, Cooper Station, New York, NY 10276 • (718)743-5229

Table of Contents

our Advantage • Getting the Most Out of the Cardoza Non-Counter Strategy •
Understanding the Gamble

IX. Money Management 67

Money Management • Emotional Control • Bankrolling:Total Bankroll • Bank-
roll Requirements • Table Bankroll • When to Quit • Minimizing Losses •
Maximizing Gains • Should You Increase Your Bet Size When Winning? • A
Winning Reminder

X. Glossary 73

53 Blackjack Terms, Jargon and Concepts Fully Defined to Make You More
Conversant With the Game

XI. Advanced Strategy Information 76

Cardoza 1, 2, 3 Multiple Deck Non-Counter • The Craps Master • The Cardoza Base Count Strategy • Home Instruction Course

List of Tables and Charts

I. Introduction to the Revised Edition

This new edition has been expanded more than 25 pages to reflect the latest information on winning money at blackjack and to show you how to beat blackjack games anywhere in the world!

We've kept the same approach that has made this book a modern classic for winning at blackjack and best-seller for more than 10 years. After clearly explaining the rules, variations and how the game is played we get right to the heart of the matter.

Winning strategies are presented three ways. First, we show the underlying principles of the strategies and explain concepts such as stiff cards, pat cards and the 10 factor.

Then, we present the strategies in mini-chart form and the thinking behind each move so that you learn why each play is made. We call this thinking process, "conceptual blackjack." Understanding why you make the plays you do, ensures that you will always make the correct plays and emerge a winner.

Finally, to make sure the winning strategies are crystal clear, we present the Cardoza Master Charts to cover the correct plays for all blackjack games wherever you may find them!

This book emphasizes winning, and that's what we're here to do now - win at blackjack!

II. Introduction

Blackjack can be beaten! Once you've finished reading this book and learned the skills presented, you'll find that there will be one major difference between you and 95% of the other players - you'll be a winner at blackjack!

We'll teach you how to win without the blind memorization and boring tedium usually associated with learning blackjack. Our computer-tested basic strategies are carefully explained so that every play you make is easily learned. In addition, all the winning strategies are presented in easy-to-read charts.

You'll learn how to beat the single deck game without counting cards and how best to adjust your play for multiple deck games whether you're a player in Las Vegas, Northern Nevada, Atlantic City, the Mississippi riverboats and Indian reservations, or you're heading for play in Europe, Asia, the Bahamas, the Caribbean or anywhere else blackjack is found.

You'll receive a wealth of information from this book. We cover the fundamentals of casino blackjack - the rules of the game, the player's options, the variations offered in casinos around the world, how to bet, casino jargon, how to play and everything else you'll need to know about playing winning casino blackjack.

Not only will we teach you the skills of winning, but just as important, we'll teach you how to walk away a winner. Money management is carefully explained to insure your success as a blackjack player. We also discuss emotional control, how to minimize losses when losing, and how to let your winnings ride, so that when you lose, you lose small, and when you win, you win big - the overall result being that you walk away a winner!

For the first time, the winning concepts that have been successfully taught at the Cardoza School of Blackjack are now presented here so that you can win without counting cards.

So read this book carefully, and you'll be among those players that the casinos fear, and for good reason - you will be a consistent winner at blackjack!

III. Beginners Guide to Casino Blackjack

Object of the Game
The player's object in casino blackjack is to beat the dealer. This can be achieved in two ways:

1 - When the player has a higher total than the dealer without exceeding 21.

2 - When the dealer's total exceeds 21 (assuming the player has not exceeded 21 first).

In casino blackjack, if the player and the dealer both hold the same total of 21 or less, the hand is a **push**, nobody wins.

Busting or Breaking - Automatic Losers
If the drawing of additional cards to the initial two cards dealt causes the point total to exceed 21, then that hand is said to be **busted,** an automatic loss. Busted hands should be turned up immediately. Once the player has busted, his hand is lost, even if the dealer busts as well afterwards. If the dealer busts, all remaining players automatically win their bets.

Blackjack - Automatic Winner
If the original two card hand contains an Ace with any 10 or face card (J,Q,K), the hand is called a **blackjack,** or **natural,** and is an automatic winner for the player whose bet is paid of at 3 to 2. If the dealer gets a blackjack, all players lose their bets. (The dealer wins only the player's bet, not the 3 to 2 payoff the player receives for a blackjack.) If both the dealer and the player are dealt a blackjack, the hand is a push. Blackjacks should be turned up immediately.

Payoffs
All bets are paid off at even money ($5 bet wins $5), except in cases where the player receives a blackjack which is a 3 to 2 payoff ($5 bet wins $7.50) or when the player exercises an

option that allows him to double his bet. In these instances (doubling and splitting), the payoff is equal to the new doubled bet. If a bet is doubled from $5 to $10, a win would pay off $10.

Card Values

Each card is counted at face value. 2=2 points, 3=3 points, 10=10 points. The face cards, Jack, Queen and King, are counted as 10 points. The Ace can be counted as 1 point or 11 points at the player's discretion. When the Ace is counted as 11 points, that hand is called **soft**, as in the hand Ace, 7 = soft 18. All other totals, including hands where the Ace counts as 1 point, are called hard, as in the hand 10, 6, A = hard 17.

The dealer must count his Ace as 11 if that gives him a hand totaling 17 to 21, otherwise he must count the Ace as 1 point.

In some casinos the rules dictate that the dealer must draw on soft 17. In these casinos, the dealer's Ace will count as 1 point when combined with cards totalling 6 points, and the dealer will have to draw until he forms a hand of at least hard 17.

Dealer's Rules

The dealer must play by prescribed guidelines. He must draw to any hand 16 or below and stand on any total 17-21. As mentioned above, some casinos require the dealer to draw on soft 17. The dealer has no options and cannot deviate from the above-stated rules.

PLAYER'S OPTIONS

Unlike the dealer, the player can vary his strategy. After receiving his first two cards the player has the following options:

1 - Drawing (Hitting)

If the player is not satisfied with his two card total he can draw additional cards. To draw a card, the player scrapes the felt surface with his cards, scraping toward his body. In a game where both the player's cards are dealt face up, the player is not supposed to touch the cards and instead scratches the felt with his index finger or points toward the cards if he desires additional cards.

2 - Standing

When a player is satisfied with his original two card total, and does not wish to draw additional cards, he signals this by sliding his cards face down under his bet. When the cards are dealt face up, the player indicates his decision to stand pat by waving is hand palm down over his cards

3 - Doubling Down

This option allows the player to double his original bet, in which case he must draw one additional card to his hand and cannot draw any additional cards thereafter. To double down, the player turns his cards face up, and places them in front of his bet. Then he takes an amount equal to his original bet and places those chips next to that bet, so that there are now two equivalent bets side by side. In games where the cards are dealt face up, the player simply places the additional bet next to his original to indicate the double down.

The dealer will then deal one card face down, usually slipping that card under the player's bet. The bettor may look at that card if he desires.

4 - Splitting Pairs

If dealt a pair of identical value cards, such as 3-3, 7-7, 8-8 (any combination of 10, J, Q, K is considered a pair), the player can split these cards so that two separate hands are formed. To split a pair, the player turns the pair face up, separates them, putting each card in its own place in front of his bet. He then places a bet equal to the original wager behind the second hand. Each hand is played separately, using finger and hand signals to indicate hitting and standing.

In games where both player cards are dealt face up, the split is indicated by placing the additional bet next to the original one, and after, using hand signals as above to indicate hitting or standing.

If the first card dealt to either split hand has a value identical to the original split cards, that card may be split again (resplit) into a third hand, with the exception of Aces. When the player splits Aces, he can receive only one card on each Ace and may not draw again, no matter what card is drawn.

5 - Doubling Down After Splitting

The player can double down on one or both of the hands resulting from a split according to the normal doubling rules of the casino. This option is offered in all Atlantic City casinos and in certain Nevada casinos. It is also found in Australia, Great Britain, various European and Asian casinos and southern Africa.

For example, if a pair of 8s are split, and a 3 is drawn to the first 8 for an 11, the player may elect to double down on that 11. He does so by placing an amount equal to the original bet next to the 11, and receives only one additional card for that hand. The other 8 is played separately and can be doubled as well should an advantageous card such as a 2 or 3 be drawn.

Since options allowed are often in flux, sometimes changing from one month to the next, when playing, check to see if this advantageous option is available.

6 - Surrender (Late Surrender)

The player may "surrender" his original two card hand and forfeit one half of his bet after it has been determined that the dealer does not have a blackjack. This option is frequently allowed in Asia and the Caribbean, while in the United States, surrender is offered in only a few casinos.

To surrender, the bettor turns both his cards face up, puts them above his bet, and says "surrender," or in a game where both player cards are dealt face up, he announces his intention verbally to the dealer.

The dealer will collect the cards and take one half of the bet.

7 - Early Surrender

A player option to give up his hand and lose half his bet before the dealer checks for a blackjack. This very favorable option was originally introduced in Atlantic City but is no longer offered because of changes in Atlantic City rules.

8 - Insurance

If the dealer shows an Ace as his upcard, he will ask the players if they want insurance. If any player exercises this option, he is in effect betting that the dealer has a 10-value card as his hole card, a blackjack. To take insurance, the player places up to one-half the amount of his bet in the area marked "insurance." If the dealer does indeed have a blackjack, he gets paid 2 to 1 on the insurance bet, while losing the original bet. In effect, the transaction is a "standoff," and no money is lost. If the dealer does not have a blackjack, the insurance bet is lost and play continues.

If the player holds a blackjack and takes insurance on the dealer's Ace, the payoff will be even-money whether the dealer has a blackjack or not. Suppose the player has a $10 bet and takes insurance for $5 on his blackjack. If the dealer has a blackjack, the player wins 2 to 1 on his $5 insurance bet and ties with his own blackjack. If the dealer doesn't have a blackjack, the player loses the $5 insurance bet but gets paid 3 to 2 on his blackjack. Either way the bettor wins $10.

Insurance Strategy

Insurance is a bad bet for the following reason:

Making an insurance wager is betting that the dealer has a 10 under his Ace. Since the insurance payoff is 2 to 1, the wager will only be a profitable option for the player when the ratio of 10s to other cards is either equal to or less than 2 to 1.

A full deck has 36 non-tens and 16 tens, a ratio greater than 2 to 1. If the first deal off the top of the deck gives us a hand of 9,7, and the dealer shows an Ace, then we know three cards, all non-tens. Now the ratio is 33 to 16, still greater than 2 to 1, still a poor bet. If you have two 10s for a 20, then the ratio is 35 to 14, an even worse bet.

In a multiple deck game, taking insurance is even a worse bet than in a single deck one.

Insuring a Blackjack

Taking insurance when you have a blackjack is also a bad bet, despite the well-intentioned advice of dealers and other players to always "insure" a blackjack. When you have a blackjack, you know three cards, your 10 and Ace, and the dealer's Ace. The already poor starting ratio of 36 tens to 16 non-tens gets worse, becoming 34 to 15 in a single deck game.

Taking insurance when you have a blackjack gives the house an 8% advantage, a poor proposition for the player.

The Play of the Game

The dealer begins by shuffling the cards and offering the cut to one of the players. If refused, it is offered to another player. The dealer then completes the cut, and removes the top card, called the **burn card**. In single and double deck games, the burn card is either put under the deck face up, where all subsequent cards will be placed, or is put face down into a plastic case (procedures vary from casino to casino) to be followed similarly by future discards.

In games dealt out of a shoe, the burn card will be placed most of the way into the shoe and discards will be put in the plastic case.

Players must make their bets before the cards are dealt

The dealer deals clockwise from his left to his right, one card at a time, until each player and the dealer have received two cards. The players cards are usually dealt face down in a single or double deck game, though it makes no difference if they are dealt face up as they usually are in a game dealt out of a shoe, for the dealer is bound by strict rules from which he cannot deviate. The dealer deals only one of his two cards face up. This card is called an **upcard**. The face down card is known as the **hole card** or the **downcard**.

If the dealer's upcard is an Ace, he will ask the players if they want insurance. Players that decide to take that option place a bet up to one-half their wager in front of their bet in the area marked insurance.

If the dealer has a blackjack, all players that did not take insurance lose their original bets. Players that took insurance break even on the play. If the dealer hasn't a blackjack, he collects the lost insurance bets and play continues.

The procedures vary when the dealer shows a 10-value card. In many Nevada casinos the dealer must check his hole card for an Ace. If he has a blackjack, it is an automatic winner for the house. All player bets are lost. (Players can't insure against a 10-value card.) Players that hold blackjack push on the play. If the dealer doesn't have a blackjack, he will face the first player and await that player's decision.

In Atlantic City, the Bahamas and most European games, the dealer will only check the hole card after all the players have acted.

Play begins with the bettor on the dealer's left, in the position known as **first base**.

The player has the option to stand, hit, double down, split (if he has two cards of equal value) or surrender (if allowed). A player may draw cards until he is satisfied with his total or busts, or he may exercise one of the other options discussed previously.

Play then moves to the next player. If any player busts (goes over 21) or receives a blackjack, he must turn over his cards immediately. If a bust, the dealer will collect the lost bet. If a blackjack, the dealer will pay the player 3 to 2 on his bet.

After the last player has acted upon his cards, the dealer will turn his hole card over so that all players can view both of his cards. He must play his hand according to the strict guidelines regulating his play; drawing to 17, then standing. (In some casinos the dealer must draw to a soft 17.) If the dealer busts, all players still in the game for that round of play win automatically.

After playing his hand, the dealer will turn over each player's cards in turn, paying the winners, and collecting from the losers. Once the bettor has played his hand, he shouldn't touch his cards again. He should let the dealer expose his hand which he will do once the dealer has played out his own hand.

When the round has been completed, all players must place a new bet before the next deal.

Casino Personnel

The casino employee responsible for the running of the blackjack game is called the **dealer**. The dealer's duties are to deal the cards to the players, and play out his own hand according to the rules of the game. He converts money into chips for players entering the game or buying in for more chips during the course of the game, makes the correct payoffs for winning hands, and collects bets from the losers.

The dealer's supervisor - technically called the **floorman**, but more commonly referred to as the **pit boss** - is responsible for the supervision of between 4-6 tables. He makes sure the games are run smoothly and he settles any disputes that may arise with a player. More importantly, his job is to oversee the exchange of money and to correct any errors that may occur.

Entering a Game

To enter a blackjack game, sit down at any unoccupied seat at the blackjack table, and place the money you wish to gamble with near the betting box in front of you and inform the dealer that you would like to get some chips for your cash. Chips may be purchased in various denominations. Let the dealer know which chips or combination of chips you'd like.

The dealer will take your money and call out the amount he is changing so that the pit boss is aware that a transaction is taking place and can supervise that exchange.

Converting Traveller's Checks and Money Order to Cash

The dealers will accept only cash or chips, so if you bring traveller's checks, money orders or the like, you must go to the area of the casino marked **Casino Cashier** to get these converted to cash. Be sure to bring proper identification to insure a smooth transaction.

Casino Chips

Standard denominations of casino chips are $1, $5, $25, $100 and for the high rollers, $500 and even $1,000 chips can sometimes be obtained. Though some casinos use their own color code, the usual color scheme of chips are: $1=silver, $5=red, $25=green and $100=black.

Betting

Casinos prefer that the players use chips for betting purposes, for the handling of money at the tables is cumbersome and slows the game. However, cash can be used to bet with, though all payoffs will be in chips.

To bet, place your chips (or cash) in the betting box directly in front of you. All bets must be placed before the cards are dealt.

House Limits

Placards located at either corner of the table indicate the minimum and maximum bets allowed at a particular table. Within the same casino you may find minimums raging from $1, $2 and $5 to other tables that require the players to bet at least $25 or $100 per hand.

At the $1, $2 and $5 tables, the house maximum generally will not exceed $500 to $1,000 while the $25 and $100 tables may allow the players to bet as high as $3,000 a hand.

Converting Chips into Cash

Dealers do not convert chips into cash. When you are ready to cash in your chips, take them to the cashier's cage where they'll be changed into cash.

Tipping

Tipping, or **toking**, as it is called in casino parlance, should be viewed as a gratuitous gesture by the player to a dealer he feels has given him good service. Toking is totally at the player's discretion, and in no way should be considered an obligation. It is not the player's duty to support casino employees.

If you toke, toke only when you're winning, and only to dealers that are friendly and helpful to you. Do not toke dealers that you don't like or ones that try to make you feel guilty about not tipping. Dealers that make playing an unpleasant experience for you deserve nothing.

The best way to tip a dealer is to place a bet for the dealer in front of your own bet, so that his chances of winning that toke are tied up with your hand. If the hand is won, you both win together; if the hand is lost, you lose together. By being partners on the hand, you establish camaraderie with the dealer. Naturally, he or she will be rooting for you to win. This is the best way to tip, for when you win, the dealer wins double - the tip amount you bet plus the winnings from that bet.

Cheating

It is my belief that cheating is not a problem in the major American gambling centers, though I would not totally eliminate the possibility. If you ever feel uncomfortable about the honesty of a game, stop playing. Though you probably are being dealt an honest game, the anxiety of being uncomfortable is not worth the action.

Do not confuse bad luck with being cheated, or a dealer's mistake as chicanery. Dealers have a difficult job and work hard. They are bound to make honest mistakes. If you find yourself shorted on a payoff, bring it immediately to the dealer's attention and the mistake will be corrected.

Free Drinks and Cigarettes

Casinos offer their customers unlimited free drinking while playing at the table. In addition to alcoholic beverages, a player can order milk, soft drinks, juices or any other beverages. This is ordered through and served by a cocktail waitress.

Cigarettes and cigars are also complimentary and can be ordered through the cocktail waitress.

The Decks of Cards

Nevada casinos use one, two, four, six and sometimes as many as eight decks of cards in their blackjack games. Often, within the same casino, single and multiple deck games will be offered.

Typically though, outside of Nevada, multiple deck blackjack dealt out of a shoe is the standard of play in the world whether played in Atlantic City, Europe, Asia, South America, the Bahamas, the Caribbean, on casino boats, or anywhere else blackjack may be found.

When one or two decks are used, the dealer holds the cards in his hand. When more than two decks are used, the cards are dealt from a rectangular plastic or wooden device known as a **shoe**. The shoe is designed to hold multiple decks of cards, and allows the cards to be easily removed one at a time by the dealer.

Each deck used in blackjack is a standard pack of 52 cards, consisting of 4 cards of each value, Ace through King. Suits have no relevance in blackjack. Only the numerical value of the cards count. Thus, for example, if four decks are used, there will now be 16 cards of each value in play, and similarly, if six decks are in play, there will be 24 cards of each value.

Standees

In some areas around the world, most notably Europe and Asia, **standees**, players not occupying a seat and betting spot at the table, are allowed to place bets in the boxes of players already seated. However, standees must accept the seated player's decision and are not allowed to advise or criticize the play made.

No Hole Card Rule

The predominant style of play in casinos outside the United States is for the dealer to take his second card after all the players have acted upon their hands. In some cases, the dealer may deal himself the card as in the U.S. casinos, but will not check a 10 or an Ace for blackjack until after the bettors have finished playing their hands.

The disadvantage to the player is that on hands doubled or split, the additional moneys bet will be lost if indeed the dealer has a blackjack. As you'll see, we'll adjust our strategies accordingly when playing in no hole card games, being less aggressive in doubling and splitting situations, so as to minimize the negative effect of this rule.

(In Atlantic City and some Nevada casinos, blackjack is played in this style. The difference in these games though, is that when the dealer has a blackjack, the player's additional bets on doubles and splits are returned. Only the original bet will be lost. Thus, this style is not a disadvantage to players.

It is only when our additional bets are not returned as in the regular no hole card games, that we adjust strategies.)

IV. Rules and Variations of the Casino Centers

Blackjack can be found all over the world, and though basically the same wherever played, the rules and variations vary from country to country, from casino to casino within a country, and sometimes, they even differ within a casino itself.

NEVADA RULES

The Las Vegas Strip rules are advantageous to the player and gives one a slight edge on the single deck game if our strategies are followed. The rule exceptions noted in Downtown Las Vegas and in Northern Nevada games are slightly disadvantageous to the player, but these can easily be overcome by using the winning techniques presented later.

Las Vegas Strip Rules
- Dealer must draw on all totals of 16 or less, and stand on all totals of 17-21.
- Player may take insurance on a dealer's Ace.
- Insurance payoffs are 2 to 1.
- Player receives a 3 to 2 payoff on his blackjack.
- Player may double down on any initial two card combination.
- Identical pairs may be split, resplit, and drawn to as desired with the exception of split Aces, on which the player is allowed only one hit on each Ace.
- One, two, four and bigger deck games are standard.

Downtown Las Vegas Rules
Rules are the same as the Las Vegas Strip rules with one exception:
- Dealer must draw to soft 17.
- One, two, four and bigger deck games are standard.

Northern Nevada Rules

Same as Las Vegas Strip rules with two exceptions:
- Dealer must draw to soft 17.
- Doubling is restricted to two card totals of 10 and 11 only.
- One, two, four and bigger deck games are standard.

ATLANTIC CITY RULES

The New Jersey Casino Control Commission regulates the rules and variations allowed in Atlantic City casinos, and Atlantic City clubs must abide by the following guidelines:
- Dealer must draw to all totals 16 or less,
  and stand on all totals of 17-21.
- Player may take insurance on a dealer's Ace.
  Insurance payoffs are 2 to 1.
- Player receives a 3 to 2 payoff on his blackjack.
- Player may double on any initial two card combination.
- Identical pairs may be split but not resplit.
- Doubling after splitting allowed.
- Four, six and eight decks are standard

EUROPEAN RULES

Blackjack is offered in numerous countries around Europe with the rules and variations changing slightly from place to place. However, the following conditions apply in a good many of these places.
- Dealer must draw to all totals 16 or less,
  and stand on all totals of 17-21.
- Player may take insurance on a dealer's Ace.
- Insurance payoffs are 2 to 1.
- Player receives a 3 to 2 payoff on his blackjack.
- Doubling Down on 9-11 Only
- Standees Permitted
- No Hole Card Rule
- 4-6 Decks Standard
- If player draws a 2 on a A8 double down hand,
  total counts as 11, not 21

RULES AROUND THE WORLD
Bahamas • Caribbean • Europe •Southern Africa • Asia • South America • Other Locations

The general blackjack variations we presented under the European Rules on the previous page are the most prevalent style of play you'll find in casinos around the world.

Sometimes you may find double after split permitted as in Great Britain, southern Africa, many European casinos and other places. In Asian and Caribbean casinos, surrender is often allowed. Anyhow, it's always a good idea to find out the particular rules of a game before playing so you know what you're up against and how best to play your hands.

(Note that single deck blackjack is hard to find or nonexistent outside the Nevada casinos. Multiple deck blackjack is the predominant style of play in casinos around the world.)

However, no matter where you play, the game of blackjack is basically the same give or take some minor options, and we'll show you how to win against any variation.

V. General Strategic Concepts

The Dealer's Only Advantage

Before we examine the correct strategies of play, it would be instructive to look at a losing strategy. In this strategy, the player will mimic the dealer; he'll draw on all totals 16 or less, and stand on all totals 17-21.

The player doing this figures that, since this strategy wins for the dealer, it must be effective for the player as well. After all, the dealer and the player will get the same number of good hands and the same number of poor hands. And if we draw just as the dealer draws, we must come out even, mustn't we?

No. As a matter of fact, the player will be playing at about a 5 1/2% disadvantage to the house. The "Mimic the Dealer" strategy overlooks one important thing. The player must act upon his hand first.

The dealer's only advantage lies in the fact that once the player has busted, the player's bet is automatically lost, regardless of the outcome of the dealer's hand. While both the dealer and the player will bust equally following these drawing-to-17 guidelines (about 28% of the time), the double bust, where both the dealer and the player bust on the same round, will occur approximately 8% of the time (28% of 28% of the time or 28 x 28). And since the player acted first, this 8% of the time (the double bust) will be the house advantage.

When we adjust for the 3 to 2 bonus the player receives on blackjacks, a bonus the house does not enjoy, we find the house enjoying a 5 1/2% edge over the player that follows the "Mimic the Dealer" Strategy.

Overcoming the Disadvantage of Acting First

In the "Mimic the Dealer" strategy we played our hands as if our goal was to get as close to 21 as reasonably possible by using 17 as a cut-off point for drawing. But this losing strategy misstates the goal of the player. In blackjack, the object is to beat the dealer. Our chances of winning are not determined by how close our total approaches 21 as the other strategy assumed, but on how good our total is compared to the dealer's total.

We can overcome the disadvantage of having to act first by making judicious use of the options available to us as a player. Not only should we double down, split pairs, hit, stand and surrender (if allowed), but we can use our knowledge of the dealer's exposed upcard to fully capitalize on these options. Needless to say, adjusting our strategy according to this knowledge of the dealer's upcard will vastly improve on the "Get as Close to 21 - Mimic the Dealer" strategy, and completely eliminate the house edge.

To Beat the Dealer

There are two factors that affect our chances of winning; the strength of our total and the strength of the dealer's total. To beat the dealer, we must know how strong our total is compared to the dealer's total so that we know if drawing additional cards or exercising a player option is a viable consideration. In addition, we must be aware of the factors that influence the final outcome of these totals so that we can determine the optimal way to play our hand.

In determining the best way to play our hand, we must know how good our total is as it stands. Do we have the expectancy of winning by standing? If so, can we increase this expectancy by drawing additional cards or by exercising a doubling or splitting option when applicable? If we do not have the expectancy of winning by standing, will the drawing of additional cards or the employment of the doubling or splitting option increase our chance of winning?

Since our object is to beat the dealer, to answer the question "how strong is our total?" we need to ask ourselves if the dealer's expectancy, judged by the information we get from his exposed card, is greater than our total.

Being able to see the dealer's upcard gives us a great deal of information about the strength of the hands that the dealer is likely to make, and we can use that information to our advantage.

The Ten Factor

The most striking feature of blackjack is the dominant role that the 10 value cards (10, J, Q, K) play - what we call the **ten factor**.

Each ten and face card is counted as 10 points each in blackjack, and the player is four times more likely to draw a 10 than any other individual card since all the other value cards, Aces through nines, consist of only four cards each as opposed to sixteen 10s. Collectively, the 10s constitute just under 1/3 of the deck (16 out of 52 cards).

Because the 10s are such a dominant factor in a deck of cards, it's correct to think of the dealer's hand as *gravitating* toward a total 10 points greater than his exposed upcard. When I speak of a hand as gravitating toward a total, I am referring to the tendency of that hand to increase in value by 10 points as a result of the 10 factor. Thus, for example, starting out with an upcard of 9, the dealer will make a hand of 19 about 36% of the time and 19 or better 52% of the time.

UNDERSTANDING THE DEALER'S UPCARD

Being able to see the dealer's upcard is of great value to the player, for there are two factors - the rules governing the dealer's play of his hand, and the number of tens in a deck of cards (ten factor) - that tell us a great deal about the potential strength of the dealer's hands, and the frequency with which those hands will bust.

The Dealer's Rules and the Ten Factor

Our strategy is based on the fact that the dealer must play by prescribed guidelines from which he cannot deviate. He must draw to all totals 16 or below, and stand on all totals 17-21 (except in casinos that require the dealer to draw to soft 17). All hard totals that exceed hard 21 are automatic dealer losses.

By combining our knowledge of the 10 factor with the above mentioned dealer rules gives us a natural separation of the dealer's upcard into two distinct groupings: 2s through 6s, the dealer "stiff" cards, and 7s through As (Aces), the dealer "pat" cards.

We'll base our strategies accordingly.

2s through 6s - Dealer Stiff Cards

Whenever the dealer shows a 2, 3, 4, 5 or 6 as an upcard, we know that he must draw at least one additional card regardless of the value of his hole card (unless the dealer has an Ace under his Six and is playing Las Vegas Strip, Atlantic city or European style rules which require the dealer to stand on soft 17). The high concentration of 10s in the deck make it likely that the dealer will expose a 10 as his hole card, giving him a stiff total of 12-16.

Since the dealer must draw to all hard totals 16 or below, the drawing of a 10 (and in some instances, smaller totalled cards) will bust any of these stiff totals. For example, if the dealer shows a 6 and reveals a 10 in the hole, any card higher than a 5 will bust his hand.

Thus, the high concentration of 10 value cards in the deck tells us that the dealer has a good chance of busting when his upcard is a 2, 3, 4, 5 or 6.

7s through As - Dealer Pat Cards

Whenever the dealer shows a 7, 8, 9, 10 or A as an upcard, we know, because of the large number of 10s, that he has a high likelihood of making pat totals 17-21, and conversely, a smaller chance of busting than when he shows a stiff card. This high concentration of 10s makes it likely that the dealer will expose a 10 for an automatic pat hand (17-21). Even when he hasn't a 10 in the hole, combinations such as 89; A7; 99 and so forth, give him an automatic pat hand as well.

Chart 1
Understanding the Dealer's Stiff Cards

Dealer Stiff Cards - Advantageous for Player

2	3	4		5	6
Less Advantageous				More Advantageous	

Dealer's Upcard of 2 and 3

Though it is favorable for the player when the dealer shows a 2 or 3 as an upcard, we will need to be cautious against these stiff cards, for the dealer will bust less often with these than when he shows the 4, 5 and 6.

Dealer's Upcard of 4, 5 and 6

The dealer is showing the upcards you always want him to hold. The dealer will bust about 42% of the time with these upcards (5% more than the 2, 3 and about 18% more than with the pat cards). We will take advantage of these weak dealer upcards by aggressive splitting and doubling.

Chart 2
Understanding the Dealer's Pat Card's

Dealer Pat Cards - Disadvantageous for Player

7	8	9		10	Ace
Moderately Disadvantageous				Very Disadvantageous	

Dealer's Upcard of 7 and 8

While the dealer will not bust often with these upcards, they also indicate to us that the dealer's hands gravitate toward the weaker totals of 17 and 18. It is interesting to note that of all the dealer upcards including the stiff cards, the 7 will form the weakest totals.

Dealer's Upcard of 9, 10 and Ace

The 9 and 10 gravitate toward totals of 19 and 20 respectively - tough hands to beat. The Ace is also a powerful dealer upcard, for in addition to forming strong hands, the dealer will bust less with an Ace than with any other upcard.

Against these powerful upcards, we will be very cautious in our doubling and splitting strategies.

UNDERSTANDING THE PLAYER'S HAND - HARD TOTALS

The player's totals can be divided into three distinct groupings: 11 or less, 17-21 and 12-16.

We will look at each in turn to see how they affect our strategy, but first, let's examine the player's pat hand totals to get a better feel for the reasoning behind the strategy plays we'll make.

Chart 3
Understanding the Player's Pat Hand Totals

<u>17</u>	<u>18</u>	<u>19</u>	<u>20</u>	<u>21</u>
poor	fair	good	excellent	excellent

When you realize that overall, the dealer will average better than an 18 for each hand played, you see why the final total of 18 is classified in our index as no better than a fair total, and that 17, is quite clearly a poor one. The total of 19 is a good hand, while 20 and 21, as all blackjack player's know, are excellent totals that we'd love to have hand after hand.

Player's Hand of 11 or Less - (Hard Totals)
We should always draw to any hard total 11 or less (unless a doubling or splitting option is more profitable). By hitting this hand we have no risk of busting, no matter what we draw, and the drawing of a card can strengthen our total.

There is no question about the correct decision; drawing is always a big gain.

Player's Hand of 17-21 - (Hard Totals)
We should always stand on these hard totals (17-21), for the risk of busting is too high to make drawing worthwhile. It should be obvious that the chances of improving these high totals are minimal, and the risks of busting very probable. In addition, totals of 19, 20, and 21 are already powerful hands, while 18, to a lesser extent, is a good playable total.

On the other hand, while hard 17 is a poor player total, the risk of busting by drawing is way too costly to make drawing a viable option.

Stand on hard totals of 17-21 against any dealer's upcard.

Player's Hand of 12-16 - (Hard Totals)
With these hands the bulk of our decision making will be exercised, for on these hard totals there are no automatic decisions as on the other player totals.

Our hand is not an obvious draw (such as the 11 or less

grouping) for the risk of drawing a 10 or other high card and busting is substantial. Our hand is not an obvious stand decision either (such as the 17-21 grouping), for the only times we will win with these weak totals of 12-16 are the times that the dealer busts.

We discuss this grouping in the following chapter, the *Optimal Basic Strategies*, where we show you the correct way to play every hand dealt in blackjack, and after, in *The Winning Edge* chapter, show you how to use this information to be a winner at blackjack.

For those players desiring an even greater edge and more profits, the mail order strategies presented at the end of the book are the next step forward for you as a successful winning player.

However, for the Cardoza Non-Counter winning strategies to be effective (or any other strategy for that matter) and for you to be a winner at blackjack, you must first know the correct way to play your hands so read the following chapters carefully.

Let's get to it!

VI. The Optimal Basic Strategies

Hitting and Standing - Hard Totals
These strategies are applicable for single and multiple deck games in all casino centers.

General Principles -
1. When the dealer shows a 7, 8, 9, 10 or A, hit all hard totals of 16 or below (unless doubling or splitting is more profitable - in any case, you will always draw a card).

2. When the dealer shows a 2, 3, 4, 5 or 6, stand on all hard totals of 12 or more. Do not bust against a dealer stiff card. Exception - Hit 12 vs. 2, 3.

Chart 4
All Casino Centers
Hitting and Standing - Hard Totals

	2	3	4	5	6	7	8	9	10	A
11/less	H	H	H	H	H	H	H	H	H	H
12	H	H	S	S	S	H	H	H	H	H
13	S	S	S	S	S	H	H	H	H	H
14	S	S	S	S	S	H	H	H	H	H
15	S	S	S	S	S	H	H	H	H	H
16	S	S	S	S	S	H	H	H	H	H
17-21	S	S	S	S	S	S	S	S	S	S

H = Hit   **S** = Stand

In all our charts, the dealer's upcard is indicated by the horizontal numbers, (running left to right) on the top row, and the player's hand is indicted by the vertical numbers (up and down) in the left column. The letters in the matrix indicate the correct strategy play.

CONCEPTUAL HITTING AND STANDING STRATEGY

In the "Understanding the Player's Hand" section we discussed the strategy for hard totals of 11 or less, and for hard totals 17-21.

They will be reiterated briefly here.

- 11 or less - Draw against all dealer upcards.
- 17-21 - Stand against all dealer upcards.

Hard Totals 12-16

It is when we hold hard totals 12-16 (stiffs) that the player's big disadvantage of having to go first (the only built-in house advantage) is a costly proposition. If we draw to hard totals and bust, we are automatic losers. But, on the other hand, if we stand, we will win with these weak totals only when the dealer busts.

It is important to realize that the decision to hit or stand with hard totals 12-16 is a strategy of minimizing losses, for no matter what we do, we have a potentially losing hand against any dealer upcard. Do not expect to win when you hold a stiff. However, in order to maximize the gain from our overall strategy, we must minimize the losses in disadvantageous situations (as above), and maximize our gains in advantageous ones.

a. Player Totals of 12-16 vs. Dealer Pat Cards 7, 8, 9, 10, A

When the dealer's upcard is a 7 through an Ace, you should expect the dealer to make his hand, for he will bust only about one time in four, a mere 25% of the time. If we stand on our hard totals 12-16, we will win only the times that the dealer busts.

Thus, for every 100 hands that we stand with our stiff totals 12-16 against dealer pat cards, our expectation is to lose 75 of those hands and to win only 25, a net loss of 50 hands. Not an exciting prognosis.

On the other hand, drawing to our stiff totals 12-16 against the dealer pat cards gives us a big gain over standing. By drawing, we will gain an average of 15%. The dealer makes too many hands showing a 7, 8, 9, 10 or Ace, to allow us to stand with our stiffs.

You will bust often when drawing to your stiffs, but do not let that dissuade you form hitting your stiffs against pat cards. The strategy on these plays is to minimize losses. We cannot afford to stand and sacrifice our bet to the 3 out of 4 hands that the dealer will make.

When the dealer shows a 7, 8, 9, 10, or Ace, hit all hard totals 16 or below.

b. Player Totals of 12-16 vs. Dealer Pat Cards 2, 3, 4, 5, 6

The greater busting potential of the dealer stiff cards makes standing with hard player totals of 12-16 a big gain over drawing. While we will win only 40% of these hands (the times that the dealer busts), standing is a far superior strategy to drawing, for we will bust too often drawing to our own stiffs against upcards that will bust fairly often themselves. The times that we would make pat totals by drawing wouldn't guarantee us winners either, for the dealer will often make equal or better totals.

On these plays, our disadvantage of having to go first makes drawing too costly, for once we bust, we automatically lose. Though the dealer will make more hands than bust, our strategy here is to minimize losses so that when we get our good hands, we'll come out an overall winner.

Exception - Hit Player 12 vs. 2, 3

Hitting 12 vs. 2, 3 is the only basic strategy exception to drawing with a stiff total against a dealer's stiff upcard. The double bust factor is not as costly on these plays, for only the 10s will bust our 12. Similarly, the dealer will bust less often showing a 2 or a 3 than with the other stiff cards, 4, 5 and 6.

This is in contrast to the play 13 vs. 2 where the correct strategy is to stand. The additional player busting factor of the 9 makes the player slightly better off by standing, even though the dealer will bust less with a 2 as an upcard. This clearly illustrates the greater importance of the player's busting factor (compared to the dealer's busting factor) when deciding whether to stand or draw with a stiff total 12-16 vs. a dealer stiff upcard.

The combination of the player being less likely to bust (more likely to make his hand) and the dealer being more likely to make his hand (less likely to bust) makes drawing 12 vs 2, 3 the correct strategy play.

Hitting and Standing - Soft Totals

The strategy for hitting and standing with soft totals in Northern Nevada and Europe is identical to the Atlantic City and Las Vegas strategies for both single and multiple deck, except that the Atlantic City and Las Vegas basic strategy players can take advantage of the more liberal doubling rules.

As a result, they will double down on hands that Northern Nevada and European Style rules players cannot.

Chart 5
Northern Nevada & Europe
Single & Multiple Deck • Hitting and Standing - Soft Totals

	2	3	4	5	6	7	8	9	10	A
A2-A6	H	H	H	H	H	H	H	H	H	H
A7	S	S	S	S	S	S	S	H	H	H
A8-A9	S	S	S	S	S	S	S	S	S	S

H = Hit   S = Stand

Chart 6
Atlantic City and Las Vegas
Single & Multiple Deck • Hitting and Standing - Soft Totals

	2	3	4	5	6	7	8	9	10	A
A2-A5	H	H	D *	D	D	H	H	H	H	H
A6	D *	D	D	D	D	H	H	H	H	H
A7	S	D	D	D	D	S	S	H	H	H
A8	S	S	S	S	S	S	S	S	S	S
A9	S	S	S	S	S	S	S	S	S	S

H = Hit   S = Stand   D = Double

* Do not double A2 or A3 vs. 4 in a multiple deck game.

* Do not double A6 vs. 2 in a multiple deck game.

CONCEPTUAL HITTING AND STANDING - SOFT TOTALS

Player's Hand of A2, A3, A4, A5
Unless the player is able to double down, he should always draw a card to these hands. Standing is a poor option, for these totals will win only when the dealer busts. The player has nothing to lose by drawing (no draw can bust these totals), and may improve his total. Players that stand on these hands might just as well give the casinos their money. Draw on A2-A5 against all dealer upcards.

Player's Hand of A6, A7, A8, A9
The decision to hit or stand with soft totals 17 or higher necessitates a closer look at the strength of these totals. Unlike hard totals of 17 or more, drawing is a viable option with these soft totals. Since we have the option of counting the Ace as 1 point or 11 points, the drawing of a 10, or for that matter, the drawing of any other card, will not bust our soft totals. While we have no risk of busting, we do have the risk of drawing a weaker total, and therefore must ask the question, "How strong is our total?"

For soft totals, we want to know:
1- What are our chances of winning by standing?
2- What are the chances of improving our hand by drawing additional cards?

Player's Hand of Soft 17 (A6)
A standing total of 17 is a weak hand against all dealer upcards, including the dealer stiff cards, and in the long run is a losing total. The only time we will win with this total is when the dealer busts. Otherwise, at best we have a push.

Always draw on soft 17 no matter what the dealer shows as an upcard. (In Las Vegas and Atlantic City and other locations where allowed, the correct strategy may be to double down. See doubling section.) This standing total is so weak that attempting to improve our hand by drawing is always a tremendous gain against any upcard.

When a casino requires the dealer to draw to soft 17, it is a disadvantageous rule to the player. Though the dealer will sometimes bust by drawing to a soft 17, in the long run he will make more powerful totals and have more winners. It affects the player the same way.

Player's Hand of Soft 18

Against dealer stiff totals of 2, 3, 4, 5 and 6, standing with our 18 is a smart strategy move (unless playing Las Vegas or Atlantic City doubling rules where doubling will often be a big player gain). We have a strong total against these weak dealer upcards.

Stand against dealer upcards of 7 and 8, for our 18 is a solid hand. Against the 7, we have a winning total, and against the 8, we figure to have a potential push, as these dealer upcards gravitate toward 17 and 18 respectively. We do not want to risk our strong position by drawing.

Against the powerful dealer upcards of 9, 10, Ace, our standing total of 18 is a potentially losing hand. Normally you would think that hitting a soft 18 is only a fair total. We are not chancing a powerful total but rather attempting to improve a weak situation.

As a matter of fact, for every 100 plays (at $1 a play) that we draw rather than stand on soft 18 vs. 9 and 10, we will gain $9 and $4 respectively. You must realize that 18 vs. 9, 10, Ace is not a winning hand and since our 18 is a soft total, we have a chance to minimize losses by drawing.

Player's Hand of Soft 19 and 20

These hands are strong player totals as they stand. Do not draw any cards. We have no need of improving these already powerful totals.

DOUBLING DOWN

Doubling down is valuable option for it gives the player a chance to double his bet in advantageous situations. The only drawback to the doubling option is that the player receives one card and gives up the privilege to draw additional cards should that card be a poor draw. To determine if the doubling option will be profitable, we must weigh the benefits of doubling our bet against the drawbacks of receiving only one card.

One of the most important factors to consider when contemplating the doubling option is the 10 factor. We are more likely to draw a 10 on our double than any other card value.

Thus, doubling on a total of 11, where the drawing of a 10 gives us an unbeatable 21, is a more powerful double than an initial two card total of 9, where the drawing of 10 gives us a strong total of 19, not as powerful as the 21.

On the other hand, we would not double any hand of hard 12 or more, for the drawing of a 10 would bust our total, and we would have an automatic loser at double the bet.

The 10 factor is also an important strategic consideration, for it affects the dealer's busting potential. We double more aggressively against the weakest of the dealer stiff cards, the 4, 5 and 6, and less aggressively against the other stiff cards, the 2 and 3.

The only times we will double against the dealer pat cards are when our doubling totals of 10 and 11, hands that could turn into 20s and 21s, are powerful themselves.

SINGLE DECK DOUBLING STRATEGY

A. Northern Nevada Single Deck Doubling - The player is restricted to doubling down on two card totals of 10 and 11 only.

Chart 7
Northern Nevada
Single Deck Doubling Down

	2	3	4	5	6	7	8	9	10	A
10	D	D	D	D	D	D	D	D		
11	D	D	D	D	D	D	D	D	D	D

D = Double Down   **Blank** = Hit, Do Not Double Down

B. Las Vegas Single Deck Doubling - The player may double down on any initial two card combination.

Chart 8
Las Vegas
Single Deck Doubling Down

	2	3	4	5	6	7	8	9	10	A
62										
44/53				D	D					
9	D	D	D	D	D					
10	D	D	D	D	D	D	D	D		
11	D	D	D	D	D	D	D	D	D	D
A2			D	D	D					
A3			D	D	D					
A4			D	D	D					
A5			D	D	D					
A6	D	D	D	D	D					
A7		D	D	D	D					
A8										
A9										

D = Double Down   **Blank** = Hit, Do Not Double Down

MULTIPLE DECK DOUBLING STRATEGY

You'll notice that the doubling strategies for multiple deck play are somewhat less aggressive than the single deck game, a difference we'll discuss a little later on.

First we'll discuss Northern Nevada, where there are three changes from single deck play, then Atlantic City and Las Vegas, where there are seven differences, and finally, European style, where there are five differences in doubling strategy from single deck play.

However, only concern yourself now with the proper play for the games you'll face, and when you encounter different rules, then make the slight adjustments necessary for that game.

A. Northern Nevada: Multiple Deck Doubling - The player may double down on two card totals of 10 and 11 only.

Chart 9
Northern Nevada
Multiple Deck Doubling Down

	2	3	4	5	6	7	8	9	10	A
10	D	D	D	D	D	D	D	D		
11	D	D	D	D	D	D	D	D	D	

D = Double Down   **Blank** = Hit, Do Not Double Down

B. Las Vegas and Atlantic City: Multiple Deck Doubling - The player can double down on any initial two card combination. These strategies are valid for all multiple deck games in Atlantic City and Las Vegas.

Chart 10
Las Vegas & Atlantic City
Multiple Deck Doubling Down

	2	3	4	5	6	7	8	9	10	A
8										
9		D	D	D	D					
10	D	D	D	D	D	D	D	D		
11	D	D	D	D	D	D	D	D	D	
A2				D	D					
A3				D	D					
A4			D	D	D					
A5			D	D	D					
A6		D	D	D	D					
A7		D	D	D	D					
A8										
A9										

D = Double Down   **Blank** = Do Not Double Down

C. European Style: Multiple Deck Doubling Down - The player may double down on totals of 9, 10 and 11 only.

Due to the no hole card rules, you double down less aggressively against the dealer's 10 than in Atlantic City and Nevada games as you can see in the following chart.

Chart 11
European Style Rules
Multiple Deck Doubling Down

	2	3	4	5	6	7	8	9	10	A
9		D	D	D	D					
10	D	D	D	D	D	D	D	D		
11	D	D	D	D	D	D	D	D		
A8										

D = Double Down   **Blank** = Do Not Double Down

CONCEPTUAL DOUBLING - HARD TOTALS (11, 10, 9, 8)

These strategies are applicable to single and multiple deck games in all casino centers. Where multiple deck strategies differ from the single deck, an asterisk will denote the strategy change, and that change will be indicated.

Doubling 11*

This is the strongest doubling hand for the player and should be doubled against all the dealer upcards in a single deck game. If we draw a 10 value card on our double, we will have a 21, the strongest hand we can have. At best, the dealer can tie us.

*Do not double 11 vs. Ace in multiple deck games. In no hole card rules games, do not double against the 10 or Ace. Hit instead.

Doubling 10

This is the second strongest doubling hand for the player and should be doubled against the dealer's 2 through 9. Our hard 10 gravitates toward a 20, an overwhelmingly strong hand against these dealer upcards.

Do not double 10 against the dealer's 10 or Ace. Doubling

our hard 10 against the dealer's 10 is not a potential winner as before (against the dealer's 2 through 9), for the dealer's hand gravitates toward a 20 as well, and our possible 20 is not powerful enough to compensate for the low busting probabilities of the dealer's Ace. Giving up the option to draw an additional card should our first draw be weak is too costly on these plays.

Note: In Northern Nevada, only hard 10 and 11 can be doubled down.

Doubling 9

Double 9 against 2 through 6 only*. The high busting potential of the dealer stiff cards (2-6) makes the 9 a profitable double down. We cannot double down against any of the pat cards (7-Ace) for our win potential when we do draw the 10 (for a total of 19) is not strong enough to compensate for the times when we when we draw a poor card and cannot draw again.

*Do not double 9 vs. 2 in a multiple deck game.

Doubling 8

Doubling 8 vs. 5, 6 is a valid play in a single deck game*. Our 8 gravitates toward an 18, only a fair total. However, the very high busting potential of the dealer 5 and 6 make this double a slight gain. Our 8 is not strong enough to make doubling against the other dealer upcards a good play.

* Do not double 8 vs. any upcard in a multiple deck game.

CONCEPTUAL DOUBLING - SOFT TOTALS

The high concentration of 10s play a different role in soft doubling than in hard doubling, for instead of having a positive effect on our chances of making a good total, the drawing of 10 will not even give us a pat hand on many of these doubles.

Doubling with soft totals is generally a gain against weak dealer upcards. The 10 factor figures strongly in the dealer's chances of busting, while on the other hand, the drawing of small and medium cards will often improve our hand to a competitive and winning total.

Doubling A2, A3, A4, A5

Double A2, A3, A4 and A5 against the dealer's 4, 5 and 6*.

The very high busting probabilities of the dealer 4, 5 and 6 makes doubling with our A2 to A5 profitable for the player. Again, the drawing of a 10 value card does not help our total, but the high dealer busting factor gives us an edge.

We do not double against the 2 and 3, because the dealer will make just too many hands with these upcards. The same is more strikingly true with the dealer pat cards, 7 through Ace.

* Do not double A2 or A3 vs. 4 in a multiple deck game.

Doubling A6

Double A6 vs. dealer 2, 3, 4, 5 and 6*. The A6 is a more powerful double than the A2-A5, for the drawing of a 10 to the A6 will at least give us a pat total and a potential push against a dealer's 17. This "push" factor enables us to gain by doubling against the dealer's 2 and 3 despite the fact that they will make more dealer pat totals than with the weaker upcards 4, 5 and 6.

* Do not double A6 vs. 2 in a multiple deck game.

Doubling A7

Double A7 vs. 3, 4, 5 and 6. Our soft 18 is only a fair total and drawing an additional card won't risk the destruction of a powerful total such as a 19 or 20.

Soft 18 is a strong double against the weaker dealer stiffs 4, 5 and 6, but differs from the soft 17 in that we do not double against the 2. A standing total of 18 vs. a 2 is a stronger winning hand and we do not want to risk the weakening of this hand by doubling and having to draw a card.

Doubling A8, A9

We have two very strong totals here and do not want to risk our excellent chances of winning by attempting to double.

Stand with these powerful hands - do not double.

SPLITTING PAIRS

Splitting can do two valuable things. It can turn one poor total into two stronger hands, such as splitting a hard 16 (8-8) into two hands of 8 each, and it effectively doubles our bet.

The decision to split requires a closer look at our hand vs. the dealer's hand, for we must balance the standing total of our hand against the two proposed split hands, and see if the split and resultant doubling of our bet increases our expectation of winning.

Here's our thought process:

1- How strong is our total as it stands.

Is the hand too powerful a total as it stands to risk breaking up? If not, we can consider the split.

2- How strong are the two proposed split totals?

Thinking in terms of the 10 factor, we want to see if our split totals gravitate toward strong totals relative to the strength of the dealer's upcard, or if the split totals represent an improvement over the hard standing original hand.

3- Does splitting either increase our chances of winning or reduce our rate of loss?

Obviously, this is an important factor as well.

SPLITTING PAIRS - SINGLE DECK BASIC STRATEGY

These strategies are applicable to all Northern Nevada and Las Vegas single deck games.

Chart 12
Northern Nevada & Las Vegas
Single Deck Splitting Pairs

	2	3	4	5	6	7	8	9	10	A
22		spl	spl	spl	spl	spl				
33		spl	spl	spl	spl					
66	spl	spl	spl	spl	spl					
77	spl	spl	spl	spl	spl	spl				
88	spl	spl	spl	spl	spl	spl	spl	spl	spl	spl
99	spl	spl	spl	spl	spl		spl	spl		
AA	spl	spl	spl	spl	spl	spl	spl	spl	spl	spl

spl = Split   **Blank** = Do Not Split
Do not split 44, 55, 10s.   Always split 88, AA

SPLITTING PAIRS - MULTIPLE DECK BASIC STRATEGY

We will split slightly less aggressively against a multiple deck game than against a single deck game especially when the game is played by the No Hole Card rules. On the other hand, when the game offers doubling after splitting, we get more aggressive.

What happens when a multiple deck game offers doubling after splitting? We'll cover each of the possibilities in turn, showing you the best way to play no matter the situation.

A. Las Vegas and N. Nevada Multiple Deck Splitting - The standard game allows pair splitting on any two cards but does not allow doubling after splitting. (If the particular game allows doubling after splitting, use the chart following this one.)

Chart 13
Las Vegas & Northern Nevada
Multiple Deck Splitting Pairs

	2	3	4	5	6	7	8	9	10	A
22			spl	spl	spl	spl				
33			spl	spl	spl	spl				
66		spl	spl	spl	spl					
77	spl	spl	spl	spl	spl	spl				
88	spl	spl	spl	spl	spl	spl	spl	spl	spl	spl
99	spl	spl	spl	spl	spl		spl	spl		
AA	spl	spl	spl	spl	spl	spl	spl	spl	spl	spl

spl = Split   **Blank** = Do Not Split
Do not split 44, 55, 10s.   Always Split 88, AA

B. Atlantic City Multiple Deck Splitting (and Nevada casinos that offer doubling down after splitting) - Because of the doubling after splitting rule, the player will split pairs more aggressively so that he can take advantage of good doubling situations that may arise as a consequence of the split.

Chart 14
Atlantic City
Multiple Deck Splitting Pairs

	2	3	4	5	6	7	8	9	10	A
22	spl	spl	spl	spl	spl	spl				
33	spl	spl	spl	spl	spl	spl				
44				spl	spl					
66	spl	spl	spl	spl	spl					
77	spl	spl	spl	spl	spl	spl				
88	spl	spl	spl	spl	spl	spl	spl	spl	spl	spl
99	spl	spl	spl	spl	spl		spl	spl		
AA	spl	spl	spl	spl	spl	spl	spl	spl	spl	spl

spl = Split
Do not split 55, 10s.

Blank = Do Not Split
Always split 88, AA

C. European Style Splitting - Players will split less aggressively than the Atlantic City (and certainly the Nevada) casinos due to the no hole card rule. This chart assumes that doubling after splitting is not allowed.

Chart 15
European Style Rules
Multiple Deck Splitting Pairs

	2	3	4	5	6	7	8	9	10	A
22			spl	spl	spl	spl				
33			spl	spl	spl	spl				
66		spl	spl	spl	spl					
77	spl	spl	spl	spl	spl	spl				
88	spl	spl	spl	spl	spl	spl	spl	spl		
99	spl	spl	spl	spl	spl		spl	spl		
AA	spl	spl	spl	spl	spl	spl	spl	spl	spl	

spl = Split
Blank = Do Not Split
Do not split 44, 55, 10s.

D. European Style - Doubling After Splitting Allowed - Many international casinos allow doubling after splitting. When this option is available, you will take advantage of it by splitting more agressively. ·

Chart 16
European Style Rules
Splitting Pairs • Doubling After Splitting Allowed

	2	3	4	5	6	7	8	9	10	A
22	spl	spl	spl	spl	spl	spl				
33	spl	spl	spl	spl	spl	spl				
44				spl	spl					
66	spl	spl	spl	spl	spl					
77	spl	spl	spl	spl	spl	spl				
88	spl	spl	spl	spl	spl	spl	spl	spl		
99	spl	spl	spl	spl	spl		spl	spl		
AA	spl	spl	spl	spl	spl	spl	spl	spl	spl	

spl = Split   **Blank** = Do Not Split
Do not split 55, 10s.

CONCEPTUAL SPLITTING

We will examine the decision to split 99 first, for it is a good example of the thinking process involved in splitting. First of all, we should note that this hand totaling 18 is only "fair," not a powerful total like a 19 or 20.

Splitting 9s - Dealer shows a 2, 3, 4, 5, 6

Split 99 against these dealer stiff cards. Our 18 is a winner, but splitting the hand into two halves of 9 each is a big gain. Each starting hand of 9, because of the 10 factor, gravitates toward strong player totals of 19.

The high busting potential of the dealer stiff cards gives us an excellent opportunity to maximize our gain in an advantageous situation.

Splitting 9s - Dealer shows a 7

Stand with 99 vs. dealer 7. We figure the dealer for a 17. Our standing total of 18 is a stronger total and a big potential winner. While splitting 9s will also produce a positive expectation of winning, the risking of our fairly secure 18 against the 7 for two strong but chancy totals reduces the gain.

We have the dealer beat. Stand.

Splitting 9s - Dealer shows an 8

Splitting 99 against the dealer's 8 is a big gain.

Against the dealer's 8, we figure our 18 to be a potential push. However, by splitting the 18 into two separate hands of 9 each, we hope to turn our potential push into two possible winners. (Each 9 gravitates toward a total of 19, one point higher than the dealer's 18.)

Splitting 9s - Dealer shows a 9

Splitting 99 vs. the dealer's 9 is also a big gain.

Against the 9, our 18 is a losing total, but splitting the 18 into two totals of 9 each reduces our potential loss. Rather than one losing total of 18, we will have two hands gravitating toward potential pushes.

Splitting 9s - Dealer shows a 10 or Ace

Do not split 99 against the dealer's 10 or Ace.

Our split hands of 9 each gravitate toward good totals, but against these more powerful dealer upcards, splitting would be a poor play. We do not want to make one loser into two.

Splitting 22 and 33

Split 22 vs. dealer 3 through 7*
Split 33 vs. dealer 4 through 7*

The high busting probabilities of the dealer 4, 5 and 6 makes the 22 and 33 good splits. We split 22 vs. 3 and not 33 vs. 3, because of the lower player busting factor of our split hands of 2 each. The drawing of a 10 gives us another chance to improve on our 2, for correct basic strategy is to draw 12 vs. 3, while the drawing of a 10 on our 3 forces us to stand.

We do not split 22 or 33 vs. the dealer's 2, because the

dealer's 2 does not bust often enough to make splitting a profitable play.

Splitting 22 and 33 vs. 7 seems unusual at first, for this play seems to exceed our normal strategic boundaries of making aggressive plays against the weak dealer stiff cards. Though the 7 is a pat card and will make a lot of pat hands, the 7 will also make the weakest totals, only gravitating toward a total of 17. Our starting totals of 2 and 3 will make hands of 18 or better about one-half the time. Splitting 22 and 33 against the dealer's 7 will not make us money (because of the high busting factor of our hands), but they will produce a moderate gain over drawing to these hands.

Do not split 22 and 33 against the 8, 9, 10 or Ace. We do not want to make one loser into two losers.

*Nevada multiple deck exception - Do not split 22 vs. 3.

*Atlantic City multiple deck exception (and games with doubling after splitting allowed) - Split 22 and 33 vs. 2 through 7.

Splitting 4s

Do not split 44*. The hard total of 8 gravitates toward a total of 18, a far better position than two weak starting totals of 4 each. Against the dealer stiff cards, 2 through 6, we have a big gain by drawing to our 8. While the drawing of 10 will not give us an overwhelmingly strong total, an 18 is far better than drawing the same 10 to a split 4.

We do not want to hold two weak hands of 4 each against the dealer pat cards, especially the dealer's 7 and 8, where we have a good starting total of 8.

*Atlantic City exception (and games with doubling after splitting allowed) - Split 44 vs. 5 and 6. The added possibilities of being able to double our bet should either or both of the split totals pull well makes this split an advantageous move.

Splitting 55

Never split 55. 55 by itself is an excellent starting total of 10. You do not want to break up this powerful player total into two terrible hands of 5 each. (Our 10 is an excellent doubling hand against dealer upcards of 2 through 9.)

Splitting 66

Split 66 against dealer stiff cards 2 through 6 only*. Our hard total of 12 is not very favorable, nor are the split hands of 6 and 6 too promising either. We have a losing hand either way against all dealer upcards. However, we want to minimize our losses.

Against the dealer stiff cards 2, 3, 4, 5 and 6, our split hands of 6 and 6 will sometimes draw cards to give us some pat totals 17-21.

Of course, we will often end up with stiff totals on the split pair (by the drawing of a 10 or other sufficiently large card) and be forced to stand. But the high dealer busting factor makes splitting 66 against the dealer stiffs a slight gain.

Obviously we will not split 66 against the dealer pat cards. We don't need two hands of 16 against a card that will bust only one time in four.

*Nevada multiple deck exception - Do not split 66 vs. 2.

*Atlantic City multiple deck (and games with doubling after splitting allowed) - No exceptions. Split 66 vs. 2-6.

Splitting 77

Split 77 against dealer upcards of 2, 3, 4, 5, 6 and 7. Against the dealer stiff cards 2 through 6, two playable hands of 7 and 7 are preferable to one stiff total of 14. Splitting 77 is not a strong split, for these totals only gravitate toward a 17, but the high busting rate of the dealer stiff cards makes this split a big gain.

Splitting 77 against the dealer's 7 is also an excellent split, for we are taking one losing total of 14 into two potential pushes of 17 each.

We do not split 77 vs. the dealer's 8, 9, 10, Ace, for we do not want to take one poor total of 14 into two hands gravitating toward a second best total of only 17.

Splitting 88

Split 88 against all dealer upcards. Against the dealer's 2 through 8, we are taking one terrible hand of 16 into two play-able totals of 8 each. There is a tremendous gain on all these plays.

Splitting 88 against the dealer's 9, 10, A are the strangest of the basic strategy plays. Using all of the intuitive knowledge we have developed, at first glance we would reason that this is a poor split, for we are making two losers out of one. However, more is involved in this play.

First, you must realize that the player hand of 16 is the worst total possible. While splitting this 16 into two hands of 8 and 8 is not a winning situation against the strong dealer upcards of 9, 10 and A, it is an improvement over our very weak total of hard 16.

Bear with this unusual play, for computer simulation studies have played out the hand millions of times for both drawing and splitting, and found that the player loses less by splitting 88. Realize that although the split is weak, it does produce a gain over drawing to our easily bustable 16.

In games employing the no hole card rule, do not split 8s against the dealer's 10 and Ace. With the possibility of the dealer getting a blackjack, we don't need more money out on this hand. Hit instead.

Splitting 10,10

Do not split 10s. The hard total of 20 is a winning hand against all dealer upcards. Splitting 10s against any dealer up-card is a terrible play, for you are taking one "solid" winning hand into two good but uncertain wins. Too often, the splitting of 10s will draw low cards, in effect destroying a great hand.

Splitting AA

Split AA against all dealer upcards. Each Ace is a powerful starting total of 11 points. If we draw the 10, our 21 can't be beat. Splitting AA is a tremendous gain against all dealer up-cards.

In no hole card rule games, we will not split Aces when the dealer shows an Ace. The high likelihood of the dealer getting a blackjack when he already has an Ace is too costly for us to double our bet. Draw instead.

VII. The Master Charts

Chart 17
Master Chart
Northern Nevada • Single Deck

	2	3	4	5	6	7	8	9	10	A
7/less	H	H	H	H	H	H	H	H	H	H
8	H	H	H	H	H	H	H	H	H	H
9	H	H	H	H	H	H	H	H	H	H
10	D	D	D	D	D	D	D	D	H	H
11	D	D	D	D	D	D	D	D	D	D
12	H	H	S	S	S	H	H	H	H	H
13	S	S	S	S	S	H	H	H	H	H
14	S	S	S	S	S	H	H	H	H	H
15	S	S	S	S	S	H	H	H	H	H
16	S	S	S	S	S	H	H	H	H	H
A2	H	H	H	H	H	H	H	H	H	H
A3	H	H	H	H	H	H	H	H	H	H
A4	H	H	H	H	H	H	H	H	H	H
A5	H	H	H	H	H	H	H	H	H	H
A6	H	H	H	H	H	H	H	H	H	H
A7	S	S	S	S	S	S	S	H	H	H
A8	S	S	S	S	S	S	S	S	S	S
A9	S	S	S	S	S	S	S	S	S	S
22	H	spl	spl	spl	spl	spl	H	H	H	H
33	H	H	spl	spl	spl	spl	H	H	H	H
66	spl	spl	spl	spl	spl	H	H	H	H	H
77	spl	spl	spl	spl	spl	spl	H	H	H	H
88	spl	spl	spl	spl	spl	spl	spl	spl	spl	spl
99	spl	spl	spl	spl	spl	S	spl	spl	S	S
AA	spl	spl	spl	spl	spl	spl	spl	spl	spl	spl

H = Hit   **S** = Stand   **D** = Double   **spl** = Split
Do not split 44, 55 (double on 55) and 10s. Always split 88 and AA

Chart 18
Master Chart
Las Vegas • Single Deck

	2	3	4	5	6	7	8	9	10	A
7/less	H	H	H	H	H	H	H	H	H	H
62	H	H	H	H	H	H	H	H	H	H
44/53	H	H	H	D	D	H	H	H	H	H
9	D	D	D	D	D	H	H	H	H	H
10	D	D	D	D	D	D	D	D	H	H
11	D	D	D	D	D	D	D	D	D	D
12	H	H	S	S	S	H	H	H	H	H
13	S	S	S	S	S	H	H	H	H	H
14	S	S	S	S	S	H	H	H	H	H
15	S	S	S	S	S	H	H	H	H	H
16	S	S	S	S	S	H	H	H	H	H
A2	H	H	D	D	D	H	H	H	H	H
A3	H	H	D	D	D	H	H	H	H	H
A4	H	H	D	D	D	H	H	H	H	H
A5	H	H	D	D	D	H	H	H	H	H
A6	D	D	D	D	D	H	H	H	H	H
A7	S	D	D	D	D	S	S	H	H	H
A8	S	S	S	S	S	S	S	S	S	S
A9	S	S	S	S	S	S	S	S	S	S
22	H	spl	spl	spl	spl	spl	H	H	H	H
33	H	H	spl	spl	spl	spl	H	H	H	H
66	spl	spl	spl	spl	spl	H	H	H	H	H
77	spl	spl	spl	spl	spl	spl	H	H	H	H
88	spl	spl	spl	spl	spl	spl	spl	spl	spl	spl
99	spl	spl	spl	spl	spl	S	spl	spl	S	S
AA	spl	spl	spl	spl	spl	spl	spl	spl	spl	spl

H = Hit **S** = Stand **D** = Double **spl** = Split
Do not split 44, 55 (double on 55) and 10s. Always split 88 and AA

Single and Multiple Deck Blackjack Differences

As we have seen, the main variations in strategy take place with our doubling and splitting strategies - moves which entail an increased wager on the hand. Let's now see just why the single and multiple deck blackjack games are slightly different.

The greater number of cards used in a multiple deck game makes the removal of any particular card or cards less important for composition change purposes and, as a result, our doubling and splitting strategies are less aggressive.

For example, the removal of three cards (5,3,5) creates a favorable imbalance for the player in a single deck game and makes a 53 double vs. the dealer's 5 a profitable play. Not only will these cards be poor draws for the player's double but they're three cards the dealer needs to improve his hand. The effective removal of these three cards gives the player a better chance of drawing a 10 on his 8 and, at the same time, increases the dealer's chance of busting. In a single deck game, 53 vs. 8 is a favorable double.

However, the removal of these three cards are barely felt in a multiple deck game. There are twenty nine other 3s and 5s in a four deck game as compared to only five in a single deck. Thus, no favorable imbalance has been created in the multiple deck game, and the double down is not a correct play.

This lack of sensitivity to particular card removal accounts for nine strategy changes in the multiple deck game from the preceeding single deck master charts we just presented.

Except for the following nine changes in the doubling and splitting strategies, multiple deck basic strategy is identical to the single deck basic strategy.

<u>**In a multiple deck game:**</u>

- 1- Do not double hard 8 vs. 5; hit instead
- 2- Do not double hard 8 vs. 6; hit instead
- 3- Do not double hard 9 vs. 2; hit instead.
- 4.-Do not double hard 11 vs. Ace; hit instead.
- 5- Do not double A2 vs 4; hit instead.
- 6- Do not double A3 vs. 4; hit instead.
- 7- Do not double A6 vs 2; hit instead
- 8- Do not split 22 vs. 3; hit instead
- 9- Do not split 66 vs. 2; hit instead

Chart 19
Master Chart
Northern Nevada • Multiple Deck

	2	3	4	5	6	7	8	9	10	A
7/less	H	H	H	H	H	H	H	H	H	H
8	H	H	H	H	H	H	H	H	H	H
9	H	H	H	H	H	H	H	H	H	H
10	D	D	D	D	D	D	D	D	H	H
11	D	D	D	D	D	D	D	D	D	H
12	H	H	S	S	S	H	H	H	H	H
13	S	S	S	S	S	H	H	H	H	H
14	S	S	S	S	S	H	H	H	H	H
15	S	S	S	S	S	H	H	H	H	H
16	S	S	S	S	S	H	H	H	H	H
A2	H	H	H	H	H	H	H	H	H	H
A3	H	H	H	H	H	H	H	H	H	H
A4	H	H	H	H	H	H	H	H	H	H
A5	H	H	H	H	H	H	H	H	H	H
A6	H	H	H	H	H	H	H	H	H	H
A7	S	S	S	S	S	S	S	H	H	H
A8	S	S	S	S	S	S	S	S	S	S
A9	S	S	S	S	S	S	S	S	S	S
22	H	H	spl	spl	spl	spl	H	H	H	H
33	H	H	spl	spl	spl	spl	H	H	H	H
66	H	spl	spl	spl	spl	H	H	H	H	H
77	spl	spl	spl	spl	spl	spl	H	H	H	H
88	spl	spl	spl	spl	spl	spl	spl	spl	spl	spl
99	spl	spl	spl	spl	spl	S	spl	spl	S	S
AA	spl	spl	spl	spl	spl	spl	spl	spl	spl	spl

H = Hit   **S** = Stand   **D** = Double   **spl** = Split
Do not split 44, 55 (double on 55) and 10s. Always split 88 and AA

Chart 20
Master Chart
Las Vegas • Multiple Deck

	2	3	4	5	6	7	8	9	10	A
7/less	H	H	H	H	H	H	H	H	H	H
8	H	H	H	H	H	H	H	H	H	H
9	H	D	D	D	D	H	H	H	H	H
10	D	D	D	D	D	D	D	D	H	H
11	D	D	D	D	D	D	D	D	D	H
12	H	H	S	S	S	H	H	H	H	H
13	S	S	S	S	S	H	H	H	H	H
14	S	S	S	S	S	H	H	H	H	H
15	S	S	S	S	S	H	H	H	H	H
16	S	S	S	S	S	H	H	H	H	H
A2	H	H	H	D	D	H	H	H	H	H
A3	H	H	H	D	D	H	H	H	H	H
A4	H	H	D	D	D	H	H	H	H	H
A5	H	H	D	D	D	H	H	H	H	H
A6	H	D	D	D	D	H	H	H	H	H
A7	S	D	D	D	D	S	S	H	H	H
A8	S	S	S	S	S	S	S	S	S	S
A9	S	S	S	S	S	S	S	S	S	S
22	H	H	spl	spl	spl	spl	H	H	H	H
33	H	H	spl	spl	spl	spl	H	H	H	H
66	H	spl	spl	spl	spl	H	H	H	H	H
77	spl	spl	spl	spl	spl	spl	H	H	H	H
88	spl	spl	spl	spl	spl	spl	spl	spl	spl	spl
99	spl	spl	spl	spl	spl	S	spl	spl	S	S
AA	spl	spl	spl	spl	spl	spl	spl	spl	spl	spl

H = Hit   **S** = Stand   **D** = Double   **spl** = Split
Do not split 44, 55 (double on 55) and 10s. Always split 88 and AA

Atlantic City Multiple Deck

The blackjack games offered in Atlantic City differ from the Nevada games in several ways. For one thing, all the Atlantic City games are dealt from either a 4, 6 or 8 deck shoe. They do not offer single or double deck games as in Nevada. Doubling allowed after splitting is standard in Atlantic City as opposed to Nevada, where only a few casinos offer this option. Resplitting of pairs is not allowed in Atlantic City. Nevada casinos generally allow the player to resplit pairs as often as they wish.

The Atlantic City game is singular in some other ways as well. To protect against collusion between the player and the dealer, the dealer does not check his hole card for a blackjack (as is standard in Nevada) until all the players have finished playing out their hands. This casino safeguard does not affect the player's chances of winning, for if the dealer does indeed have a blackjack, any additional money the player may have wagered on a doubled or split hand will be returned. Only the original bet is lost.

Another difference is that all player hands are dealt face up in Atlantic City. No casinos allow the player to physically handle the cards. The player must employ hand signals to convey his strategy intentions to the dealer. (Single and double deck games in Nevada are generally face down games where the player can handle his cards, while multiple deck games are played similarly to the Atlantic City face up game.)

The Atlantic City basic strategy is the same as Nevada multiple deck strategy except for more frequent pair splitting due to the player being allowed to double after splits.

European No Hole Card Rules

These strategies are for multiple deck play and take into account that players may only double on totals of 9, 10 and 11, and also will double and split less aggressively when the dealer shows a 10 or Ace due to the no hole card rule.

In no hole card games that allow the player to double after splitting, the player will split more aggressively to take advantage of this favorable option. We'll also show that strategy in a master chart.

Chart 21
Master Chart
Atlantic City • Multiple Deck

	2	3	4	5	6	7	8	9	10	A
7/less	H	H	H	H	H	H	H	H	H	H
8	H	H	H	H	H	H	H	H	H	H
9	H	D	D	D	D	H	H	H	H	H
10	D	D	D	D	D	D	D	D	H	H
11	D	D	D	D	D	D	D	D	D	H
12	H	H	S	S	S	H	H	H	H	H
13	S	S	S	S	S	H	H	H	H	H
14	S	S	S	S	S	H	H	H	H	H
15	S	S	S	S	S	H	H	H	H	H
16	S	S	S	S	S	H	H	H	H	H
A2	H	H	H	D	D	H	H	H	H	H
A3	H	H	H	D	D	H	H	H	H	H
A4	H	H	D	D	D	H	H	H	H	H
A5	H	H	D	D	D	H	H	H	H	H
A6	H	D	D	D	D	H	H	H	H	H
A7	S	D	D	D	D	S	S	H	H	H
A8	S	S	S	S	S	S	S	S	S	S
A9	S	S	S	S	S	S	S	S	S	S
22	spl	spl	spl	spl	spl	spl	H	H	H	H
33	spl	spl	spl	spl	spl	spl	H	H	H	H
44	H	H	H	spl	spl	H	H	H	H	H
66	spl	spl	spl	spl	spl	H	H	H	H	H
77	spl	spl	spl	spl	spl	spl	H	H	H	H
88	spl	spl	spl	spl	spl	spl	spl	spl	spl	spl
99	spl	spl	spl	spl	spl	S	spl	spl	S	S
AA	spl	spl	spl	spl	spl	spl	spl	spl	spl	spl

H = Hit   **S** = Stand   **D** = Double   **spl** = Split
Do not split 55 and 10s. Always split 88 and AA.

Chart 22
Master Chart
European No Hole Card Style • Multiple Deck

	2	3	4	5	6	7	8	9	10	A
7/less	H	H	H	H	H	H	H	H	H	H
8	H	H	H	H	H	H	H	H	H	H
9	H	D	D	D	D	H	H	H	H	H
10	D	D	D	D	D	D	D	D	H	H
11	D	D	D	D	D	D	D	D	H	H
12	H	H	S	S	S	H	H	H	H	H
13	S	S	S	S	S	H	H	H	H	H
14	S	S	S	S	S	H	H	H	H	H
15	S	S	S	S	S	H	H	H	H	H
16	S	S	S	S	S	H	H	H	H	H
A2	H	H	H	H	H	H	H	H	H	H
A3	H	H	H	H	H	H	H	H	H	H
A4	H	H	H	H	H	H	H	H	H	H
A5	H	H	H	H	H	H	H	H	H	H
A6	H	H	H	H	H	H	H	H	H	H
A7	S	S	S	S	S	S	S	H	H	H
A8	S	S	S	S	S	S	S	S	S	S
A9	S	S	S	S	S	S	S	S	S	S
22	H	H	spl	spl	spl	spl	H	H	H	H
33	H	H	spl	spl	spl	spl	H	H	H	H
66	H	spl	spl	spl	spl	H	H	H	H	H
77	spl	spl	spl	spl	spl	spl	H	H	H	H
88	spl	spl	spl	spl	spl	spl	spl	spl	H	H
99	spl	spl	spl	spl	spl	S	spl	spl	S	S
AA	spl	spl	spl	spl	spl	spl	spl	spl	spl	H

H = Hit   **S** = Stand   **D** = Double   **spl** = Split
Do not split 44, 55 and 10s

Chart 23
Master Chart
European No Hole Card: Doubling After Splitting Allowed

	2	3	4	5	6	7	8	9	10	A
7/less	H	H	H	H	H	H	H	H	H	H
8	H	H	H	H	H	H	H	H	H	H
9	H	D	D	D	D	H	H	H	H	H
10	D	D	D	D	D	D	D	D	H	H
11	D	D	D	D	D	D	D	D	H	H
12	H	H	S	S	S	H	H	H	H	H
13	S	S	S	S	S	H	H	H	H	H
14	S	S	S	S	S	H	H	H	H	H
15	S	S	S	S	S	H	H	H	H	H
16	S	S	S	S	S	H	H	H	H	H
A2	H	H	H	H	H	H	H	H	H	H
A3	H	H	H	H	H	H	H	H	H	H
A4	H	H	H	H	H	H	H	H	H	H
A5	H	H	H	H	H	H	H	H	H	H
A6	H	H	H	H	H	H	H	H	H	H
A7	S	S	S	S	S	S	S	H	H	H
A8	S	S	S	S	S	S	S	S	S	S
A9	S	S	S	S	S	S	S	S	S	S
22	spl	spl	spl	spl	spl	spl	H	H	H	H
33	spl	spl	spl	spl	spl	spl	H	H	H	H
44	H	H	H	spl	spl	H	H	H	H	H
66	spl	spl	spl	spl	spl	H	H	H	H	H
77	spl	spl	spl	spl	spl	spl	H	H	H	H
88	spl	spl	spl	spl	spl	spl	spl	spl	H	H
99	spl	spl	spl	spl	spl	S	spl	spl	S	S
AA	spl	spl	spl	spl	spl	spl	spl	spl	spl	H

H = Hit   **S** = Stand   **D** = Double   **spl** = Split
Do not split 55 and 10s

Player's Options

Use these strategies where the following options are permitted:

Chart 24: Doubling Down Permitted After Splitting

A standard option in Atlantic City, Great Britain and many casinos around the world, but offered only in a few Nevada casinos. It allows the player to double down on one or more of the hands resulting from a split according to the standard doubling rules of the casino. This option allows us to split more aggressively so that we may take advantage of good doubling situations that can arise as a consequence of the split. This option is favorable to the player.

Our Hand		Single Deck	Multiple Deck
22	split against	2-7	2-7
33	split against	2-7	2-7
44	split against	4-6	5-6
66	split against	2-7	2-6
77	split against	2-8	2-7

Chart 25: Late Surrender (Surrender)

A player option to forfeit his hand and lose half his bet after it has been determined that the dealer does not have a blackjack. This option is favorable to the player.

Our Hand		Single Deck	Multiple Deck
16*	surrender against	10, A	9,10, A
15	surrender against	10	10
77	surrender against	10	-

* Do not surrender 88 (split)

Chart 26: Early Surrender

A player option to forfeit his hand and lose half his bet *before* the dealer checks for a blackjack. A rare option, but extremely valuable for the player if available.

Dealer's Upcard		Player's Totals
A	early surrender with	5-7, 12-17
10	early surrender with	14-16
9	early surrender with	16*

Do not surrender soft totals   *Do not early surrender 88 (split)

VIII. The Winning Edge

The removal of cards from play and the continued dealing from a deck depleted of these played cards, creates situations in blackjack where the odds of receiving particular cards or combinations of cards constantly change. Computer studies have found that the proportionate removal of certain cards gives the player an advantage over the house, while the proportionate removal of others gives the house an advantage over the player.

Thus, as cards are removed from play, the player's chances of winning constantly change. Sometimes the depleted deck of cards will favor the house and sometimes the player.

By learning to analyze a depleted deck of cards for favorability, and capitalizing on this situation by betting more when the remaining cards are in your favor, you can actually have an edge over the casino.

The heart of all winning systems at blackjack is based on this theory - betting more when you have the advantage, and less when the house has the advantage. This way, when you win, you win more, and when you lose, you lose less. Beginning with an even game (playing accurate basic strategy), this "maximize gain, minimize loss" betting strategy will give you an overall edge on the house.

How do we determine when we have the edge?

Computer studies have determined that 10s and Aces are the most valuable cards for the player, while the small cards, 2 through 7, are the most valuable cards for the house, 8s and 9s being relatively neutral.

Off the top of the deck, with all cards still in play, the player has an even game with the house - neither side enjoys an advantage.*

*Assuming the player plays perfect basic strategy as we've shown, and that the game is a single deck game with the favorable Las Vegas Strip rules. If the particular game has less liberal rules (Northern Nevada) or is a multiple deck game, the house enjoys a slight initial edge.

The odds shift in favor of the player when there is a higher ratio of 10s and As in the deck than normal, and shift in favor of the house when there is a higher ratio of small cards, 2s through 7s, than normal.

All counting systems base their winning strategies on keeping track of the ratio of high cards to low cards. The systems vary in complexity from the very simple to the very complicated, all being based on the same principle - betting more when there is a higher proportion of 10s and Aces in the deck, and less when there is a higher proportion of low cards, 2 through 7s, remaining.

However, there are many blackjack players that wish to have an edge over the house but are loathe to learn counting systems. For the player that desires to win without counting cards, the Cardoza School of Blackjack has developed some simple but effective techniques.

The Cardoza Non-Counter Strategy - Five Easy Steps

The system is simple. All you need to know is that high cards favor us and the small cards favor the house. When there are more high cards in the deck than normal, you will bet more.

But you need not count cards. All you need to do is to keep your eyes open and watch the cards, just as you probably do anyway.

Following are five easy guidelines for the non-counter to enjoy an edge over the casino:

One. When a great many small cards have been played in the first round, it is to the player's advantage. Bet 3 or 4 units instead of your normal 1 or 2 unit bet. (If $5 is your standard bet, then $15 is considered a 3 unit bet)

Example - The following cards have been played. You had an 8, 5, 6, the player to your left had 10, 6, 2, another player had 10, 6, 5 and the dealer had a 10, 7. A disproportionate number of small cards have been played, meaning the remaining cards are richer in high cards - to the player's advantage. So you bet more.

Two. If on succeeding rounds, you estimate that there are still a disproportionate number of high cards remaining, continue to bet at a higher level than your minimum or neutral bet. Through practical experience, you will be able to improve on your estimation abilities.

Three. If the cumulative distribution of cards seems to be fairly normal after a round of play, bet your neutral or minimum bet. (1 or 2 units, whatever your preference is.) If, however, you notice that no Aces have appeared, increase your bet by one unit. Your potential to get a blackjack has increased. While the dealer's chances of getting a blackjack has increased as well, he only gets paid even-money; you get paid 3 to 2.

Four. On the other hand, if a disproportionate number of high cards appear in the first round, then place your minimum 1 unit bet, for the house has an edge. And if on succeeding rounds you judge that there is still a disproportionate number of small cards remaining, continue to place your minimum bets.

Five. If the cumulative distribution of cards appears to be normal and you notice that more Aces have appeared than what you normally would expect (one Ace for every 13 cards is the normal composition), you want to downgrade your bet to one unit if you had been making 2 unit bets.

Quick Summary of the Five Winning Principles
When there are more 10s and Aces remaining in the deck than normal, increase your bet. When there are fewer 10s and Aces than normal (meaning more small cards), decrease your bet. Every time the deck is shuffled, start your estimation of favorability over again.

Bet Range
I recommend a bet range of 1-4 units. Thus, if $5 is your standard bet, your maximum bet should not exceed $20.

This is an important guideline to adhere to for the following five reasons:

1. Your advantage will rarely be large enough to warrant a bet larger than 4 units. We have bankroll limitations to consider, and do not want greed to be our downfall. Keep in mind that blackjack is a slow grind for the good players.

2. Raising your bets in advantageous situations to a range greater than 1-4 will attract undue attention to you as a skillful player, and the casino may begin to shuffle every time you make a large bet, in effect shuffling away advantageous situations.

3. You do not want to have one extremely large losing bet destroy an otherwise good session at the table.

4. The losing of a huge bet will generally have a very detrimental effect on your confidence, your concentration and your ability to think clearly. You will be surprised at how fast this can affect your physical and psychological frame of being.

5. The ranging of your bets from 1 unit in disadvantageous situations to 4 units in highly advantageous situations is a wide enough bet spread to maximize your gains while at the same time minimizing your risk.

The Power of Our Advantage

The Cardoza Non-Counter strategy gives you an advantage powerful enough at $5-$20 hand for $100 profit expectancy in a heavy weekend of play in a single deck game, while $25-$100 hand has a $500 expectancy of winning.

The Cardoza Non-Counter strategy is most effective in single deck games, and less so in double decks ones due to the fewer number of cards. This strategy's main advantage is that it allows you to win with much less mental effort than counting systems require while having fun at the same time!

Now that you have the winning edge on the house, time will work to your advantage. The longer you play, the more money you can expect to make.

Obviously you cannot win as much without counting cards, but you can still win - with the odds!

The strategy is less effective in four, six and eight deck games where the overall number of the cards is less susceptible to composition changes from just a few cards being removed.

For multiple deck players, the news is not all bad though, for the basic strategies that we have presented in this book will bring you very close to an even game against the casino and should you ever decide to improve your game further by learning a counting strategy, what we've presented here is essential information anyway.

The optimal basic strategies for all deck games that we've presented in this book are 100% correct and the absolute best available.

Those readers desiring to further their edge over the house in blackjack, and to increase their profit expectancy, must learn either a counting system or the advanced non-counter strategy. See the back of the book for information on how to obtain the highly effective but simple to use Cardoza Base Count Strategy or the Cardoza 1, 2, 3 Multiple Deck Non-Counter.

Getting the Most Out of the Cardoza Non-Counter Strategy

For those players that will be playing in Nevada, or other areas where there is a choice, it will be to your advantage to play in a single deck game rather than a multiple deck one for the following two reasons:

1. The single deck game is inherently more favorable.

2. The Cardoza Non-Counter strategy is most effective in a single deck game because the single deck game is highly sensitive to composition changes.

For those players who are accessible only to multiple deck games, you have two choices if you want to have the advantage over a multiple deck game.

Choice number one is that you can purchase the simple-to-use Cardoza Non-Counter Multiple Deck Strategy. This will give you an edge of about 1/2 - 1%. This brand new strategy was developed for players who are intimidated by counting cards and it actually allows non-counting players the mathematical edge over the casino in multiple deck games. This strategy is our own research and is brand new.

The second choice is the Cardoza Base Count Strategy, or even better, the home instruction course, which is designed for serious players who want to work just a little harder. These card counting strategies give you an edge of from 1 to 3% over the casino and put you on a professional level of play.

These card counting strategies and the exciting new Multiple deck non-counter can be ordered through the coupons in the back of the book.

However, before anything else, you must learn the optimal basic strategies in this book if you want to be a winner. We can't stress this enough. You bought this book to be learn how to win. So let's win! Learn the strategies.

Understanding the Gamble

One of the realities of any gambling proposition is that no matter how well an individual plays a game, if chance is involved there will be times when the player will experience terrible runs of bad luck. There is no way to predict when these runs will begin, how long they will last or when they will stop.

It is important to understand that just because you have an advantage over the house, it does not mean you will win every time. Having a bad losing streak is not necessarily a reflection on your playing abilities. Even the best players take beatings on occasion. With a small advantage in blackjack, the skillful player will be vulnerable to dizzying streaks of luck, both good and bad.

However, if a skill factor is involved in the gambling proposition, as in blackjack, that factor will eventually make the skillful player a winner. In the short run, luck goes back and forth, but as more and more hands get played out, skill begins to take its due and that is why it's so important to follow our winning strategies to the letter.

The bettor that sticks by his guns when things go poorly will find tremendous rewards when things go his way, for, in the end, a player with the skills of winning will be way ahead of the game, a big winner!

IX. Money Management

Winning at blackjack requires not only the playing of the correct strategies but also the intelligent use of one's monetary resources. Blackjack is a very streaky game, and you can expect big winning and big losing streaks.

To emerge a winner from these pendulous swings of fortune takes a certain degree of emotional control, for the temptation to ride a winning streak too hard in the hopes of a big killing or to bet wildly during a losing streak, trying for a quick comeback, are two of the most common factors that destroy gamblers. Inevitably, big winning sessions dissipate into small wins or even disastrous losses while moderately bad losing sessions can turn into a nightmare.

Read this section carefully, for the difference between you ending up a winner or a loser is heavily influenced by your skills in managing your money intelligently.

Money management skills can be divided into the following three categories:
- **Emotional Control**
- **Bankrolling** (Total bankroll, table bankroll).
- **When to Quit** (Maximize gains, minimize losses).

Before we look at these skills more closely, there is one extremely important point that must be thoroughly understood.

> **Never gamble with money you cannot afford to lose either financially or emotionally.**

The importance of this rule cannot be overemphasized.

Betting with money you cannot afford to lose adversely affects decision making. Rather than playing your best game, your strategy gets restricted to the confines of your monetary or emotional situation. Betting with "scared money" is a guaranteed way to ensure yourself a losing career as a gambler.

Emotional Control

It is important to recognize that behind every bet you make is your money and your emotions, and that the ups and downs of your moods and feelings affect the quality of your play. For blackjack to be a pleasurable and successful experience every time you gamble, you must be aware of your state of mind and obey its needs.

Sometimes you won't feel 100%, perhaps a day where your confidence or alertness is low. Accept and recognize that condition. As a human being, you experience moods, and will not always feel at your best. It's important to recognize when your physical or emotional condition is affected and to refrain from playing.

Whenever you feel emotionally unprepared to risk money, again, you should refrain from playing. And if, for whatever reason, the game becomes a cause of anxiety and ceases to be a form of entertainment, than it is time to take a breather.

You won't play as well because your mind will be preoccupied by the possibility of losing and perhaps more importantly, you will receive no emotional satisfaction from the game.

Play again later on, when you're more alert and confident, and you will have the necessary ingredients of a winner - emotional control. Remember, the casinos aren't going anywhere. There's lots of time to get your bets down.

Bankrolling
A. Total Bankroll

To be a successful blackjack player, your bankroll must be large enough to withstand the normal fluctuations common to blackjack. Under-capitalization and overbetting are great dangers to the serious gambler.

The player that consistently overbets will have larger winning sessions when he wins, but when he loses, he'll lose big. If a losing streak becomes extended, that player could be wiped out.

Playing with a bankroll large enough to sustain short run swings of bad luck is the only way to insure that your skill will bear long term results.

The following bankroll requirements have been prepared to

give you enough capital to survive any reasonable losing streak, and be able to bounce back on top.

In the following table, **flat betting** refers to betting the same amount every time. When ranging bets from 1-4, you'll need a larger bankroll, for more money is wagered.

Chart 27 Total Bankroll Requirements		
Hours to Play	Bet Range	Bankroll Needed
10	Flat	50 units
20+	Flat	100 units
10	1-4	150 units
20+	1-4	200 units

If you plan on playing for an extended weekend's worth of play (20 hours or more) at $5-$20 a hand, you should bring $1,000 with you, while if you are only planning to play 10 hours at those stakes, $750 will give you a fairly safe margin.

This does not mean that you will lose this money playing $5-$20. Using the Cardoza Non-Counter betting strategy, you will have an edge on the house in a single or double deck game, and your expectancy is to win money every time you go.

However, it's important that you be aware that losing streaks occur, and that losing $500-$600 is a possibility, though a small one. If the thought of losing amounts comparable to this during a downswing scares you, you should not play $5-$20 a hand, for you're betting over your head.

Again, bet within your financial and emotional means, and you will never regret a single session at the tables.

If you have a definite amount of money to play with and want to figure out how much your unit size bet should be, simply take your gambling stake and divide it by the amount of units you need to have.

Thus, if you bring $500 with you, and plan to play for 10 hours ranging your bets from 1-4, divide $500 by 150 units (see chart: bankroll needed column) and you will wager about $3 a hand. Betting more than $3 as a unit would be overbetting, and leaving yourself vulnerable to the risks discussed earlier.

B. Table Bankroll

How much money should you bring to the table?

My recommendation is that your bring 30 units to the table each time you play. If playing $5 units, bring $150; if $2 units, bring $60. $25 bettors should bring $750. $100 bettors should sit down with $3,000.

Chart 28		
Table Bankroll Recommendations		
Bet Range: 1-4 Units		
Unit Bet	**Minimum Stake**	**Maximum Stake**
$1	$20	$30
$2	$40	$60
$5	$100	$150
$10	$200	$300
$25	$500	$750
$50	$1000	$1500
$100	$2000	$3000

You can bring less if you want. If flat betting, 15 units will suffice. If your bet range is from 1-4, 20 units will do the trick. However, do not bring more money to the table. 30 units is enough to cover normal swings, and you never want to lose more than that in any one sitting.

When to Quit

What often separates the winners from the losers is - the winners, when winning, leave the table a winner, and when losing, restrict their losses to affordable amounts. Smart gamblers never allow themselves to get destroyed at the table.

As a player, you have one big advantage that, if used properly, will insure you success as a gambler - You can quit playing whenever you want to. To come out ahead, you must minimize your losses when you lose and maximize your gains when you win. This way, your winning sessions will eclipse your losing sessions and you will come out an overall winner.

Minimizing Losses

Here are three simple guidelines that, if followed, will save you a lot of money.

1. Limit your table losses to 20 units (30 at the most). If betting $5 chips, never lose more than $100 in any one session; if $2 units, then $40; if $25 units, then $500.

Do not dig in for more money, and you can never be a big loser. Take a break, try again later. You never want go get into a position where losing so much in one session totally demoralizes you.

2. Never increase your bet range beyond your bankroll capabilities. In other words, always bet within your means.

3. Never increase your bet size to catch up and break even. Raising your bets will not change the odds of the game, nor will it change your luck. What it will do is make your chances of taking a terrible beating frighteningly high.

As we discussed earlier earlier, do not get into a position where losing so much in one session destroys any reasonable chance of coming out even. You can't win all the time. Rest awhile; you'll get them later.

Maximizing Gains

Following are two tried and true steps to maximize your winning sessions at blackjack.

1. Once winning, the most important thing is to walk away a winner.

There is no worse feeling than to leave the table a loser after having been up a lot of money.

Once your wins at a table have exceeded 20 units, put aside 10 units of your winnings, and play the other 10 units. If a losing streak ensues and you lose those 10 units, you have protected yourself. You walk away with 10 units in winnings!

2. Set no limit on your winning sessions.

If your hot streak continues, keep putting wins aside into

your "don't touch" pile. When your luck changes and you have lost that 10 unit buffer, you can quit a big winner.

Should you increase your bet size when winning?

If you would like to try for a bigger win, the answer is yes, go for it - but in moderation. Do not get overzealous for that leaves your hard-earned win vulnerable to a few big losses. Increase your bets gradually when winning, keeping in mind that the more you bet, the more you risk losing.

One more thing to keep in mind. Just because you may have won six hands in a row doesn't mean that you'll win your seventh bet. You can just as easily lose that seventh hand as you could win it.

The theory on betting more at "hot" tables sounds good, but nobody has ever made a living following that strategy.

Mathematically, and in practice, only the odds of the game determines a player's chances of winning a particular play, not the won or lost results from a previous play.

A Winning Reminder

Learn your basic strategies perfectly, apply the Cardoza Non-Counter betting strategy and listen to the advice offered in this money management section and you will have the knowledge and skills to be a consistent winner at the 21 tables.

Having the advantage over the casino doesn't mean you will always win, as we discussed, but if you follow our advice to the letter, you should win a majority of the times you play, and overall be ahead of the game.

Good skill!!!

X. Glossary

Barring a Player - The exclusion of a player from the blackjack tables when casino personnel feel a player is too skillful.

Basic Strategy - The optimal playing strategy for a particular set of rules and number of decks used, assuming the player has knowledge of only his own two cards and the dealer's upcard.

Blackjack or Natural - An original two card holding consisting of an Ace and ten-value card. Also the name of the game.

Break - see Bust.

Burn Card - A card, usually form the top of the deck, that is removed from play. The top card is traditionally *burned* after a fresh shuffle and before the cards are dealt.

Bust or Break - To exceed the total of 21, an automatic loser.

Card Counting - A method of keeping track of the cards already played so that knowledge of the remaining cards can be used to adjust strategies. A player that counts cards is called a *card counter*.

Composition of the Deck - A term used to describe the particular makeup of the cards remaining in the deck.

Composition Change - As cards are removed from the deck, the normal proportion of certain cards to other groups of cards change. This is called a composition change.

Dealer - The casino employee who deals the cards, makes the proper payoffs to winning hands and collects lost bets.

Doubling, Doubling Down - A player option to double the original bet after seeing his original two cards. If the player chooses this option, one additional card will be dealt.

Doubling after Splitting - Option offered in only some United States and international casinos whereby players are allowed to double down after splitting a pair (according to normal doubling rules).

Draw - see Hit.

Early Surrender - An option to forfeit a hand and lose half the bet before the dealer checks for a blackjack.

Exposed Card - see Upcard.

Eye in the Sky - Refers to the mirrors above the gaming tables where the games are constantly supervised to protect both the player and the house from being cheated.

Face Card - Also known as **Paint**. Jack, Queen or King.

First Base - Seat closest to dealer's left. The first baseman acts upon his hand first.

Flat Bet - To bet the same amount every hand.

Hard Total - A hand without an Ace or if containing an Ace, where the Ace counts as only 1 point (10, 6, A).

Head On or Head to Head - Playing alone with the dealer.

High Roller - A player that wagers big money.

Hit - The act of drawing (requesting) a card from the dealer.

Hole Card - The dealer's unexposed downcard.

House - A term to denote the Casino.

Insurance - A side bet that can be made when the dealer shows an Ace. The player wagers up to half his original bet and gets paid 2 to 1 on that bet if the dealer shows a blackjack. If the dealer does not have a blackjack, the insurance bet is lost. Play continues as usual.

Marker - An IOU signed by a player with established credit at a casino.

Multiple Deck Game - Blackjack played with two or more decks of cards, usually referring to a 4, 6 or 8 deck game.

Natural - see Blackjack.

Nickels - $5 chips, usually red in color.

Northern Nevada - Usually referring to Lake Tahoe and Reno but can include other casino locations in Northern Nevada.

Pat Card - A dealer upcard of 7 through Ace, that tends to give the dealer pat hands.

Pat Hand - A hand totalling 17-21.

Pit Boss - Casino employee who supervises play at the gaming tables.

Push - A tie between the dealer and the player. Neither side wins.

Quarters - $25 chips, usually green in color.

Shoe - An oblong box used to hold multiple decks of cards. All 4 and 6 deck games are dealt out of a shoe.

Shuffle, Shuffling Up - The mixing of cards by a dealer prior to a fresh round of play.

Silver - $1 tokens or dollar chips.

Single Deck Game - Blackjack played from a single pack of cards.

Soft Hands, Soft Total - Hand in which the Ace counts as 11 points.

Splitting Pairs - A player option to split two cards of identical value so that two separate hands are formed. A bet equal to the original wager is placed next to the second hand.

Stand, Stand Pat - A player's decision not to draw a card.

Stiff Card - A dealer upcard of 2 through 6, that leaves the dealer with a high busting potential.

Stiff Hand - A hand totalling hard 12, 13, 14, 15 or 16; can be busted if hit.

Surrender, Late Surrender - A player option to forfeit his original hand and lose half the bet after it has been determined that the dealer does not have a blackjack. Option offered in some casinos.

Ten Factor - Refers to the concentration of tens in the deck.

Ten Poor - Refers to a low proportion of 10 value cards remaining in play.

Ten Rich - Refers to a high proportion of 10 value cards remaining in play.

Ten-Value Card - 10, Jack, Queen or King.

Third Base - Also called **Anchorman.** Position closest to the dealer's right. The third baseman makes the last play before the dealer's turn.

Toke or Tip - A gratuity either given or bet for the dealer.

Unit - Bet size used as a standard of measurement.

Upcard - The dealer's face up (exposed) card.

CARDOZA SCHOOL OF BLACKJACK
- Home Instruction Course - $200 OFF! -

At last, after years of secrecy, the **previously unreleased** lesson plans, strategies and playing tactics formerly available only to members of the Cardoza School of Blackjack are now available to the general public - and at substantial savings. **Now,** you can **learn at home,** and at your own convenience. Like the full course given at the school, the home instruction course goes **step-by-step** over the winning concepts. We'll take you from layman to **pro.**

MASTER BLACKJACK - Learn what it takes to be a **master player**. Be a **powerhouse,** play with confidence, impunity, and **with the odds** on your side. Learn to be a **big winner** at blackjack.

MAXIMIZE WINNING SESSIONS - You'll **learn how** to take a good winning session and make a **blockbuster** out of it, but just as important, you'll learn to cut your losses. Learn exactly when to end a session. We cover everything from the psychological and emotional aspects of play to altered playing conditions (through the **eye of profitability**) to protection of big wins. The advice here could be worth **hundreds (or thousands) of dollars** in one session alone. Take our guidelines seriously.

ADVANCED STRATEGIES - You'll learn the **latest** in advanced winning strategies. Learn about the **ten-factor**, the **Ace-factor**, the effects of rules variations, how to protect against dealer blackjacks, the winning strategies for single and multiple deck games and how each affects you; the **true count**, the multiple deck true count variations, and much, much more.
And, of course, you'll receive the full Cardoza Base Count Strategy package.

$200 OFF - LIMITED OFFER - The Cardoza School of Blackjack home instruction course, which is retailed at $295 (or $895 if taken through the school) is available now for just $95.

BONUS! - Rush your order in now, for we're also including, **absolutely free,** the 1,000 word essays, "How to Disguise the Fact that You're an Expert", and "How Not to Get Barred". Among other **inside information** contained here, you'll learn about the psychology of the pit bosses and receive a comprehensive guide on how they spot counters.
To order, send $95 by check or money order to:
Cardoza Publishing, P.O. Box 1500, Cooper Station, New York, NY 10276

SAVE $200!
(regular $295 - Only $95 with coupon)

Order Now! Be a big winner! Please **rush** me the course by mail. I want to join the thousands of successful graduates winning big money at blackjack. I understand that the two bonus essays will be included **absolutely free.**
Enclosed is a check or money order for $95 (plus postage and handling) made out to:

Cardoza Publishing
P.O. Box 1500, Cooper Station, New York, NY 10276

Please include $3.50 postage and handling for U.S. & Canada, other countries $7.00. Orders outside United States, money order payable in U.S. dollars on U.S. bank only.

NAME _____

ADDRESS _____

CITY _____ STATE _____ ZIP _____

Offer valid only through this coupon = 30 Day Money Back Guarantee! CBS BJ
